SACRED TRACKS

2000 Years of Christian Pilgrimage

SACRED TRACKS

2000 Years of Christian Pilgrimage

JAMES HARPUR

FRANCES LINCOLN

Frances Lincoln Limited
4 Torriano Mews
Torriano Avenue
London NW5 2RZ
www.franceslincoln.com

Sacred Tracks: 2000 Years of Christian Pilgrimage
Copyright © Frances Lincoln Limited 2002
Text copyright © James Harpur 2002
Illustrations copyright as listed on page 192

First Frances Lincoln edition 2002

British Library Cataloguing-in-Publication data
A catalogue record for this book is available from the British Library.

ISBN 0 7112 1804 8

Printed and bound in Singapore

2 4 6 8 9 7 5 3 1

PREVIOUS: A pilgrim approaches the Spanish city of Santiago de Compostela, with the
towers of the cathedral visible on the skyline; RIGHT: The adoration of Christ by the
three Magi, a relief from the lid of a third-century sarcophagus, Rome.

CONTENTS

FOREWORD

While writing this book I had the privilege of being poet-in-residence at Exeter Cathedral in Devon. During my time there I was shown an unadorned marble tomb that belonged to a fifteenth-century bishop named Edmund Lacy. The tomb's outer edge was several shades darker than the rest of its surface because, as I was told, it had been constantly touched by the fingertips of medieval pilgrims. A virtuous man while alive, Lacy had come to be venerated locally as a saint after his death. Dramatic evidence of this came to light in 1943, when war-damaged masonry above his tomb revealed a cache of wax votive offerings: miniature models of arms, legs, feet and torsos left by pilgrims to show which parts of their bodies had been healed. I could picture the medieval scene: the stalls outside the cathedral selling wax models; the pilgrims filing into the candlelit interior; and Lacy's tomb, bedecked with wax images, coins, jewels and tapers, with the sick and lame gathered round. For me, the tomb brought home the fact that all over medieval Christendom, quite apart from the major places of pilgrimage, there existed thousands of smaller, local shrines such as Lacy's, and that in pre-Reformation Europe pilgrimage was as much a part of the fabric of religion as the hypnotic tolling of a church bell. Nowadays, pilgrimage is increasingly popular among Christians. Some, like their medieval forebears, seek cures for illness; some desire to strengthen the bonds of their faith; and others journey to find a sense of connection – with the community of fellow pilgrims past and present, with themselves or with God.

Sacred Tracks describes how Christian pilgrimage began and developed, how it peaked in the Middle Ages and declined after the Reformation, and how it revived during the nineteenth and twentieth centuries. As well as sketching the historical course of pilgrimage and the events and movements that affected it, the book focuses on various aspects of pilgrimage during its medieval heyday, such as the cult of relics and the conditions of travel, and describes a number of major shrines, from medieval times to the present day. Pilgrimage is a vast subject, and I have concentrated on the

Carrying his young child and a candle, a modern-day pilgrim
makes his way to a local shrine in the city of Palermo, Sicily.

6

Christian West and in particular on places that I have either visited myself or feel an affinity for; other significant sites I have mentioned in a gazetteer at the back of the book.

I am indebted to many for the making of this book: to Eveline O'Donovan, for her help and encouragement; to Frances Lincoln, for their care and expertise; and to all the pilgrims, scholars, writers and seekers after truth who have travelled this path before me, many of whose names can be found in the bibliography. It is with humility that I cast this stone on the pilgrim cairn formed by their rocks; but I do so in the hope that some interesting threads may be picked out by this panoramic sketch of Christian pilgrimage over more than two millennia.

INTRODUCTION

The practice of pilgrimage can be traced back many centuries BC to the cultures of ancient Egypt and Greece, and is probably as old as religion, which is perhaps as old as mankind. Christian pilgrimage proper began during the first two centuries after the death of Jesus Christ, when members of the faith gathered at the tombs of saints and martyrs to honour them and pray for their intercession. After Emperor Constantine I and his successors Christianized the Roman world from the fourth century onwards, pilgrimage increased dramatically, with sites in the Holy Land and various parts of Europe receiving visitors from all around the empire. Despite waxing and waning according to historical events such as the rise of Islam, the Reformation and the growth of scepticism during the so-called Age of Reason, Christian pilgrimage has survived to the present, perhaps stronger now in some parts of Europe than it has been since the end of the Middle Ages.

Although it is possible to follow the river of Christian pilgrimage from the heights of historical perspective, it is less easy to say what exactly its waters consist of, or what makes them flow and where they will run in the future. The word 'pilgrimage' is derived from the Latin *peregrinus* (from *per*, 'through', and *ager*, 'field' or 'land') and clearly suggests the idea of a journey and of a predetermined destination. Yet there were Irish pilgrims in the early Middle Ages who set out 'for the love of Christ', without a goal, letting God guide their footsteps. Pilgrimage is often associated with going to a shrine to perform certain religious rituals. Yet many of the thousands of Christians (in name at least) who visit shrines every day in the West, who light candles, leave money and buy devotional mementoes, may well hesitate to call themselves 'pilgrims'. Conversely, some non-believers who travel to lay flowers beside the Vietnam War Memorial in Washington may feel their journey has the ritual and emotional intensity of any 'religious' pilgrimage.

Even if pilgrimage does not technically need a specific destination, it still implies a

Jerusalem, with the Dome of the Rock and the old city walls, seen at dawn from the Mount of Olives to the east of the city. Jerusalem has been a place of pilgrimage for Christians for some 2,000 years of its turbulent history.

journey, as well as, perhaps, an accompanying state of serious inner reflection – which some would term 'religious' or 'spiritual' – to distinguish it from mere travel or sightseeing. But then another question arises: does the journey have to be a physical, external one? The fifteenth-century mystic Thomas à Kempis said that no matter where a person was he or she would always be a 'stranger and pilgrim', unable to find peace unless united inwardly with Christ: for him true pilgrimage was an inner journey along the pathway of the spirit, with the living Christ as the ultimate shrine. In John Bunyan's great allegorical work *The Pilgrim's Progress*, the pilgrimage is one of overcoming moral obstacles and gaining self-knowledge in order to arrive at the Celestial City. Its readers become pilgrims in the imagination, accompanying Christian as he walks through the Valley of Humiliation, resists the temptations of Vanity Fair or escapes from Doubting-Castle.

Pilgrimage may not, then, necessitate a physical journey – for Kempis and Bunyan it is possible for the pilgrim to remain in a cloister or a prison cell. Even so, inner pilgrimage, like its external counterpart, still implies movement – towards a new spiritual state of being. Therefore, whether pilgrimage is made physically or contemplatively, the idea of journeying remains central to it: the pilgrim must make a journey because he or she needs time – time to reflect upon personal dilemmas or wrongdoings, or upon the great mysteries of life, such as fate, suffering and the nature of God. For the pilgrim the journey, with all its vicissitudes, is not the wearisome preamble to truth – it is the necessary way to truth, the living, arduous and joyful process by which truth can be attained. Pilgrimage has inherent challenges and demands, highs and lows – it is a journey not to be taken lightly. Nowadays it is possible to travel to pilgrim shrines quickly and in comfort, but many prefer to expose themselves to a slow, sacred metamorphosis, realizing that the hardship of heat, cold, rain, blisters and fatigue can open up the mind to old memories and new possibilities, and can effect an emotional and spiritual purification. The destination – the shrine, the mountain or the church – signifies not the end of the journey, but the start – a portal into a new way of being, of seeing life afresh with spiritually cleansed eyes.

The story of Christian pilgrimage could be said to start with the journey of the Magi to the Christ child. But Christian writers have also looked back to the Old Testament to find inspiration for the idea of pilgrimage in the example of Abraham, who was called upon by God to leave his home in Ur, southern Mesopotamia, to start a new life in the land of Canaan. Abraham's summons is the archetypal call of the pilgrim – the irresistible prompting to exchange the familiar with the strange, the secure with the unknown, a life of ongoing domesticity with one charged with divine meaning. The exodus of the Children of Israel from bondage in Egypt also provided a paradigm: a journey of danger and hardship, of backsliding and miraculous help, and an arrival in the home promised by God – again, Canaan. For Christians the 'promised land' is heaven, and life is often viewed as a pilgrimage of the soul to this divine place or state. St Paul, in his second Letter to the Corinthians (5:1–17), said that for as long as we are alive on earth we are conscious of being absent from God, and that 'we groan, longing to be clothed with our heavenly dwelling'. The Letter to the Hebrews (11:13–16) refers to people being 'strangers', 'aliens' and 'pilgrims' on earth, longing for a 'heavenly' country. And St Augustine of Hippo in North Africa wrote that humans were like 'travellers' away from God and that to return to the true homeland – heaven – we must 'use this world, not enjoy it'.

For Christians, therefore, pilgrimage has a deep symbolic resonance that goes beyond traditional reasons for making the journey, such as performing a penance, giving thanks to God, petitioning for a cure, fulfilling a vow, reinvigorating faith and, more unofficially, experiencing the sights and sounds of foreign travel. The anthropologist Victor Turner suggested that another attraction of pilgrimage, which he likened to a rite of passage, is that it temporarily frees pilgrims of social ties and lets them experience *communitas*, or fellowship, with other pilgrims. However, underlying all these motives for Christian pilgrims is the idea that to make a journey to a sacred centre is to enact a concrete ritual representing the journey of the soul through the travails of mortal life to heaven. It is this powerful sense of a divine destiny, of an ultimate heavenly destination, that has given Christian pilgrimage its depth and universal appeal, enabling it to endure for more than two millennia with no signs of abating. For every pilgrim making a physical journey, the sore feet, enforced detours and flea-ridden hostelries, as well as the companionship and acts of generous hospitality represent in microcosm the woes and weals of life. The pilgrim's final arrival at the shrine, the source of holiness, signifies the soul's entering a state of blessedness, a rehearsal on earth for what heaven has in store. Of course, for the

pilgrim, unlike the immortal soul, there is the question of returning, a process of disengaging from the sanctified place and state, from temporary oneness with the divine, and of reintegration with the secular, the familiar world of 'home'. Yet for those pilgrims who have successfully committed themselves in thought and action to the transformatory journey, their adjustment to the quotidian will be sustained by a fresh attitude towards it, by a knowledge that they have re-enacted the journey of the soul and glimpsed the blessed state, even if only in a fragmentary way.

The aim of *Sacred Tracks* is to outline how Christian pilgrimage has fared over the last 2,000 years and to fill in some of its historical context. The first section, 'Early Paths', describes the beginning of the cult of relics and saints, especially at Rome, and how the Holy Land became the most popular pilgrim destination during the time of Emperor Constantine I. It goes on to relate how, in Dark Age Europe, Christianity blossomed in Ireland, from where a stream of pilgrims, missionaries and scholars flowed out to continental Europe; how pilgrimage was disrupted by the spread of Islam and the Viking incursions; and how conditions improved towards the end of the tenth century, when Europe became more peaceful and the Church more vital and authoritative.

The book's second section, 'Medieval Roads', begins with the new millennium and the period of the Crusades in the late eleventh and twelfth centuries. By this time

Pilgrims at prayer in the new church at Taizé in eastern France. The Brothers, clothed in white vestments, pledge themselves forever to live and work in the community.

pilgrim shrines were established all around Europe, and pilgrimage was part and parcel of religion. The section looks at some fundamental concepts of medieval pilgrimage, such as heaven, hell, purgatory and indulgences, and also at the nuts and bolts of making a journey to a shrine. It also shows that by the late Middle Ages the idea of pilgrimage was being challenged by religious critics and, in a more subtle way, by a nascent interest in travel and sightseeing – the *curiositas* that St Augustine of Hippo had railed against a thousand years before.

The third section, 'Modern Ways', traces the course of pilgrimage from the Reformation to the present. It describes how the Protestants attacked pilgrimage along with other aspects of the unreformed Church, such as rituals, relics and purgatory. As a result pilgrimage, especially in Protestant countries, declined dramatically or ceased; or it transmuted into quasi-pilgrimage activity such as the Grand Tour of the eighteenth century. Then in the nineteenth and twentieth centuries pilgrimage began to stir again, perhaps as a reaction to increasing industrialization and because of a need to supplement conventional forms of worship with a more participatory approach. New Marian shrines such as Lourdes, Knock and Fatima came into being, and there was also a revival of medieval shrines such as Walsingham. Finally, the epilogue briefly considers the direction Christian pilgrimage might take in the future, including the potential of 'virtual pilgrimage' via the Internet. Today, although the congregations of many churches in the West are suffering a decline in numbers, pilgrimage continues unabated. More pilgrims make journeys to shrines – by foot, car, coach, boat and plane – than ever before. Some of the more famous and popular destinations not included in the main body of the book are briefly described in the gazetteer at the end.

EARLY PATHS

BEGINNINGS

The first pilgrims associated with the Christian faith were arguably the Magi, the 'three wise men' who, according to the Gospel of Matthew journeyed from the east to Bethlehem, guided by a star, to pay homage to the 'one who has been born king of the Jews'. Their story contains some of the classic elements of pilgrimage. First and foremost there was a journey. In their case this would have probably been a long one from Iran, since according to the fifth-century Greek historian Herodotus the Magi were in fact a Median tribe who lived within the Persian Empire and were renowned as soothsayers and astrologers. Like pilgrims before and after them, the men were anxious to experience a source – for Christians *the* source – of sacred awe. They also wanted, in the manner of another pilgrim tradition, to pay reverence in the form of gifts: gold, incense and myrrh, which for later Christians came to symbolize respectively royalty, divinity (incense was burnt during religious ceremonies) and Jesus' passion (myrrh was used to embalm corpses).

What distinguishes the Magi's journey from most other later pilgrimages was that they came to see a living being, not the relics of someone who had died. But their instinct was the same, namely the desire for contact with a source of holiness. This was usually the first prerequisite for Christian pilgrimage – the wish to seek out a place where there was spiritual virtue, which usually took the form of the bones or other material remains of a martyr or saint. The rationale for this was that the godliness certain individuals exhibited during their lives could be transmitted through their relics and be of benefit to those who came to see and touch them. This idea in turn presupposed that inanimate objects could generate or transmit divine power. Glimpses of this belief can be seen in the New Testament. In Matthew 9:20–22 a woman suffering from a blood disorder came up behind Jesus and touched his clothing thinking to herself, 'If I only touch his cloak, I will be healed', and she was. In the Acts of the Apostles 19:12 it is said that while St Paul was residing in Ephesus in Asia Minor 'God did extraordinary miracles' through him, so that 'even

PREVIOUS: The three Magi, following the star to the birthplace of Christ, from a mosaic at St Apollinaire Nuovo, Ravenna; RIGHT: A relief from a fourth-century marble sarcophagus depicting a woman being healed by touching the cloak of Jesus.

handkerchiefs and aprons that had touched him were taken to the sick, and their illnesses were cured and the evil spirits left them'.

The cult of relics was to lie at the heart of pilgrimage; but it is not entirely clear whether members of the Church believed that spiritual energy was actually stored in the sacred objects or whether they were simply the means through which the power of God could flow, like a magnifying glass intensifying the rays of the sun. The fourth-century churchman St Cyril of Jerusalem, for instance, thought that relics were repositories of actual spiritual virtue and cited the incident in the Old Testament when the corpse of a man, accidentally put into the tomb of Elisha, sprang back to life on touching the prophet's bones. Later in the Middle Ages, St Thomas Aquinas took a different view, saying that God honoured relics by working miracles in their presence – that is, the relics were the channel for cures and miracles but did not directly cause them (see pages 67–70).

If relics or other sources of spiritual benefit were indispensable to pilgrimage, another crucial factor was a place where they could be accessed. It might be possible to obtain a cure from a living saint; but if he or she were moving about all the time it made pilgrimage difficult: the idea of pilgrimage implied a fixed destination, whether it was a tomb, a church or a grotto, and which was often itself venerated as a holy spot through having absorbed the divine energy of what it housed. In the early centuries of the Church, the tradition began of visiting the tombs of those who had been renowned for their saintliness or for their inspirational display of fortitude while being persecuted or put to death. Christian martyrs – those willing to die for the sake of Christ – went back to St Stephen, who according to Acts 6:8–7:60 was stoned to death after his fierce denunciation of the Jewish faith. The constant oppression of Christians within the Roman Empire, from Nero (37–68) to the great persecution that occurred during the reign of Diocletian (284–305) added a constant supply of martyrs to the ranks of the blessed. In fact the Romans were on the whole tolerant of other people's gods, but they generally considered Christians to be fanatical 'atheists' and made them convenient scapegoats for disasters, whether natural or manmade. The Church Father Tertullian remarked that 'if the Tiber rises too high or the Nile sinks too low, the cry is "The Christians to the lion!"'; but he also noted that the blood of the martyrs was the seed of the Church. Every Christian put to death meant another opportunity for establishing a cult and strengthening the corporate unity of the living and the dead within the Church.

THE EARLY MARTYRS

The classic example of how the relics of a martyr came to be venerated was the death in the mid-second century of St Polycarp of Smyrna in Asia Minor. This is described in a circular letter written by members of his congregation, who tell how their bishop, well advanced in age, was hunted down by the Roman authorities and taken off to the local arena and execution ground. Inside, Polycarp was given the chance to save his life by swearing allegiance to Caesar and proclaiming 'Away with the atheists [i.e. Christians]!'. Polycarp did shout out the phrase, but as he did so he gestured towards the ranks of baying pagans. He was then told to reject Christ, but he replied, famously, 'For eighty-six years I have served him, and he never did me any harm: how can I now blaspheme my King and Saviour?' Unable to break his faith or spirit, the Romans sentenced him to death by burning. But when the fire began to rage around him it suddenly took a shape 'like the sail of a ship when filled by wind' and formed a circle around the bishop, making him shine like 'gold and silver glowing in a furnace'. He was then stabbed and his body placed in the flames. 'Afterwards,' the Smyrna congregation wrote, 'we took his bones counting them more precious than the most exquisite gems and more pure than gold, and put them in a suitable place, where with joy and good cheer we shall congregate, as opportunity lets us, and the Lord shall grant us to celebrate the anniversary of his martyrdom.'

In addition to mentioning two important ingredients of pilgrimage – bones 'more precious than gems' and 'a suitable place' to keep them – the story of Polycarp also refers to a third component: a devoted group of believers ready to gather at the shrine in celebration. An idea of how the cult of the martyrs became more elaborate is suggested by the fourth-century saint Gregory of Nyssa in his address about the martyr St Theodore. In this he alludes to an 'ornate structure' that had been built over the saint's remains and also to the fact that even dust from the tomb was a 'gift and treasure'. Gregory also said that St Theodore 'attends on God', to whom he can pass on the prayers of petitioners. This was a belief that would sustain pilgrims and other members of the faith through the centuries: the saint or martyr was thought of as a friend who could intercede on behalf of the petitioner. From this it was a short step to believing that being buried near a saint would increase your chances of being received into the company of saints and the presence of God on the Day of Judgment. This in turn led Christians to lay greater emphasis on their burial rituals and their cemeteries, where during the 300s and 400s it became the practice to build elaborate tombs and to hold public worship. As one late fourth-century Christian inscription said: 'He received a tomb near the threshold of saints, something many wish for but few attain.' So the tomb of the saint became the focus for burials, for local worship and, on anniversaries, for large gatherings of the faithful – the first regular groups of Christian pilgrims. Gregory of Nyssa described the crowds flocking to Theodore's tomb to celebrate his annual festival, and depicted the road to his tomb teeming with people 'like ants, some coming and others leaving'.

THE CATACOMBS OF ROME

In the early Christian era, the most frequented pilgrimage places were in Rome, where Christians buried their dead in labyrinthine subterranean passages and chambers known as catacombs. There were also catacombs in Naples, Sicily and Malta, but Rome's were the most famous and extensive. The Roman catacombs were carved out of the *tufa* (soft porous rock), mainly around the roads that fanned out from the city. Bodies of the faithful were covered in lime, wrapped in cloth and placed in rectangular niches known as *loculi* chipped out of the sides of passages. There were also *cubicula*, or tomb chambers, for more prestigious burials or for the dead of more than one family. Christians created these underground tombs because burial was forbidden inside Rome's walls (pagan Romans usually practised cremation and

Pilgrims to the catacomb of St Priscilla, Rome, would have been greeted by this bright and welcoming wall painting depicting Christ as the Good Shepherd.

deposited the ashes of their loved ones in urns). Professional Christian diggers known as *fossores* were responsible for excavating the cemeteries, many of which lay on land given by wealthy individuals. If space was limited, the *fossores* would create galleries on different levels – sometimes up to four or five.

About forty second-century catacombs have been unearthed in Rome. Something of the atmosphere that early pilgrims experienced when visiting these underground tombs can be glimpsed from a description given by St Jerome, who lived in Rome as a boy in the mid-fourth century. Jerome used to go to the catacombs on Sunday to visit the 'tombs of apostles and martyrs'. The descent into the ground, the darkness and the recesses in the walls filled with corpses brought to his mind the words of Psalm 55:15, 'Let them go down into hell alive'. Every so often the darkness was partially dispelled by light let in through *luminaria*, light wells in the form of chimney-like shafts. Then as he moved away from the light, the darkness quickly enclosed him again, reminding him of the scene in Virgil's *Aeneid* in which the hero Aeneas searches for his wife Creüsa at night while the Greeks sack Troy – 'everywhere a sense of dread afflicted me, as did the very silence itself'.

But it would be wrong to suppose that the catacombs were merely dark, creepy dungeon-like places. The *cubicula* were like small chapels and were places of warmth and welcome, gaily painted with life-affirming scenes from the Bible expressing, for instance, belief in the Resurrection through depictions of Christ raising Lazarus from the dead; or proclaiming the ideal of Christian fellowship with murals of people eating and drinking together at funeral banquets or Eucharistic meals. Visitors came to pay their respects or to pray at the tombs of their relatives and friends (who according to the inscriptions and emblems included doctors, carpenters, smiths and bakers); or they came to celebrate the anniversaries of the martyrs with wine, bread and hymn singing, as is indicated by the remains of glass drinking vessels, decorated with gold-leaf pictures of saints and biblical scenes.

The numbers of pilgrims coming to the catacombs increased during the fourth century, when *luminaria* were first constructed to add light and improve the air supply, and stairways widened to help access. The dynamic reciprocal relationship between the living and the dead can be inferred from tomb inscriptions and graffiti left by visitors. One inscription on the tomb of a woman named Agape in the

catacomb of Priscilla asks pilgrims to 'think of your beloved Agape so that Almighty God preserves her in eternity' – an often-found plea that later theologians took as evidence of belief in purgatory (see pages 62–66). If the dead requested prayers from the living, the living requested intercession from the dead, as numerous graffiti show, for example in the catacombs of Calepodius and Callistus. Perhaps the most interesting of the pilgrims' graffiti are in the catacomb of St Sebastian on the Via Appia, which may have temporarily housed the bodies of St Peter and St Paul themselves for a number of years after 258. Why this should have been so is still a mystery, since the traditional burial places of the two apostles were well established elsewhere (Peter's on Vatican Hill and Paul's on the road to Ostia); it is possible they were moved to the catacomb for security reasons during the persecution of Emperor Valerian at this time. In any case, the apostles' connection with the site is demonstrated by more than 600 graffiti addressed to them, most with simple invocations such as 'Peter and Paul, help Primitivus a sinner' and 'Paul and Peter, pray for Victor' (pictured above left).

By the end of the fourth century the poet Prudentius was able to describe the crowds of pilgrims flocking to the tomb of the martyr St Hippolytus and to refer to the 'countless martyrs' tombs' in Rome. But as the Eternal City became prey to barbarian armies in the fifth and sixth centuries, the catacombs, unprotected by the city walls, grew less attractive as burial sites and pilgrim destinations, and gradually fell into decay. The Goths plundered them in 537 and the Lombards did the same in 756. Two years later Pope Paul I began to transfer the sacred bones of martyrs into the city, a process continued by his immediate successors. Within a few centuries the catacombs were virtually forgotten, and remained so until the fifteenth and sixteenth centuries, when the antiquarian Antonio Bosio – the 'Columbus of the catacombs' – began exploring them.

ABOVE LEFT: Graffiti in the catacomb of St Sebastian, Rome, invoking the prayers of St Peter and St Paul; RIGHT: Burial niches (*loculi*), some with their original inscriptions, lining a passage in the catacomb of Callistus, Rome.

THE AGE OF CONSTANTINE

The fortunes of the Church changed radically and permanently when the Roman general Constantine defeated his rival Maxentius in 312 – a victory apparently inspired by a vision of the cross in the sky. As emperor of the Western Roman Empire (and later the Eastern Empire) Constantine proceeded to make Christianity the most favoured religion in his dominions. From this time onwards almost every succeeding emperor was Christian, at least in name, and the bishops of Rome became increasingly influential in both the spiritual and the political spheres. Although there are doubts about his exclusive personal devotion to Christianity, Constantine took measures to elevate the status of the faith: the Church was allowed the legal right to inherit property; clergy were exempt from taxation and service in public office; celibacy was no longer subject to fiscal penalties; Sunday was made a public holiday; and state funds were made available for Church use. He himself took an avid interest in Church affairs

and presided at the Council of Nicaea in 325, at which the Arian heresy (the doctrine that held that Jesus Christ was not truly divine) was condemned. He endowed the Church with property from all over the empire, including Rome itself, where he built the Church of St Peter over the tomb or cenotaph of the apostle on Vatican Hill (see pages 94–6). He also made the ancient Greek city of Byzantium in Asia Minor his capital, renaming it Constantinople.

From the time of Constantine onwards, the Holy Land became an increasingly popular destination for pilgrims, who, as St Cyril of Jerusalem pointed out, believed they could draw nearer to God through contact with the actual places touched by Christ. Fourth-century graffiti on the walls of churches in Nazareth and Capernaum indicate that visitors came from many different parts of the empire. This surge of pilgrim activity owed much to the efforts of Constantine's mother Helena, a fervent Christian who in 326, when she was in her late seventies, set off to see the Holy Land. In Jerusalem, according to tradition, she excavated Jesus' tomb and discovered the True Cross on which he had been crucified. Part of it was kept by the Church in Jerusalem, while part was sent off to Constantinople along with the holy nails, which Constantine had fitted into his crown and his horse's bridle. Soon bits of the cross were circulating all over Christendom – Cyril of Jerusalem remarked that 'The whole world is filled with [them]'. Perhaps this was because some of the pieces were minute. St Paulinus of Nola, for example, had a splinter that was *in segmento pene atomo* – 'almost as small as an atom'.

With the enthusiasm and material support of Constantine and Helena, grand Christian churches began to rise in Palestine. Jerusalem itself now had monumental shrines befitting its central position in the Christian faith. The most important of these was the Church of the Holy Sepulchre, built on the traditional site of Jesus' execution and his burial nearby. The most resonant shrine for Christian pilgrims to this day, the church was originally a complex of buildings that featured the Anastasis ('Resurrection'), a circular, domed structure placed over Jesus' tomb, and next to it the Martyrion, a large basilica the interior of which was designed for large congregations

Detail from *The Legend of the True Cross*, a fresco by Piero della Francesca showing the authentification of the Cross by Helena, mother of Emperor Constantine.

and was richly carved and gilded. The church was twice destroyed and restored during succeeding centuries, then in the 1140s the Crusaders combined the different buildings under one roof – the plan that it still has today.

One of the first travellers to witness Constantine's building programme was the anonymous Bordeaux Pilgrim, who in 333–34 made the earliest recorded pilgrimage from the west to the Holy Land. Unfortunately, the account he – or possibly she – left is mostly an unembellished list of the stages of his journey, which if a little monotonous at least shows the impressive imperial network of roads and hostels. From Bordeaux he made his way to Toulouse and Valence before crossing the Alps into Italy. From there he travelled through the Balkans to Constantinople, then rode south through what is now Turkey and Syria to Jerusalem. (For the record, he covered 3,250 miles, made 190 stops and changed horses 360 times.) In Jerusalem the pilgrim mentions a number of sights that would be familiar to visitors in later times. He refers, for instance, to the 'pinnacle of the Temple', which Satan tried to tempt Jesus to jump off; the column against which Jesus was scourged; and the recently finished Church of the Holy Sepulchre, 'of wondrous beauty', along with its external water tanks and 'bath' for baptizing infants. His guides also showed him, perhaps more controversially, the very palm tree whose branches were used to strew the path of Jesus as he made his triumphal entry into Jerusalem. He also visited the nearby village of Bethany, where Jesus raised Lazarus from the dead, the ruins of the city of Jericho and the Dead Sea – a curiosity for pilgrims down the ages – whose water was 'very bitter' and without fish, and 'if anyone dives in for a swim, the water turns him over'.

For the rest of the fourth century, under Constantine's successors, the Church continued to expand and consolidate – the only fly in the ointment being Julian the Apostate, who tried unsuccessfully to re-establish paganism as the state religion. But the Church was too well entrenched for what Athanasius, bishop of Alexandria, called 'a little cloud and it will soon pass'. It was more preoccupied with theological disputes – such as debates about the nature of Christ in relation to the Father – which were often fuelled by regional politics. Paganism suffered a further blow during the reign of Theodosius I (379–95), who destroyed temples and outlawed sacrifices (though pagans themselves were tolerated). By the time of his death Christianity was not just the favoured imperial faith: the Roman state was a Christian state.

The Solitaries

While the Church as an institution was becoming part of the imperial establishment, attracting money, property and endowments from the wealthy, there was a counter-movement in which a good number of Christians turned their backs on the world and, to deepen their spirituality, embraced an ascetic life as monks and hermits, attracting pilgrims in the process. Influential among these early solitaries was St Antony of Egypt (*c.* 251–356), the patron saint of monks, whose reputation for holiness was such that even while alive he himself became the object of pilgrimage. Born in Upper Egypt, Antony withdrew from society in 269 to live with local ascetics and copy their way of life. In 286 he retreated to a deserted fortress on a mountain near the east bank of the Nile and lived there for twenty years, periodically struggling with demons in the form of wild beasts. Despite his isolation, Antony's reputation as a holy man spread abroad, drawing pilgrims to his lonely outpost. At first he refused to see them, but many made their homes in huts and nearby caves and begged him to be their spiritual guide. Eventually, in about 305, Antony succumbed to their request and for the next five years taught and organized them into a loose-knit community obedient to a monastic rule. In about 310 he again retreated into solitude, this time to a mountain near the Red Sea, where he spent the remaining years of his long life.

Another ascetic of this early period who attracted pilgrims during his lifetime was St Simeon Stylites (390–459), the famous 'pillar hermit'. Born in northern Syria, Simeon entered a monastery near Antioch in his teens then left to become a solitary in a remote hut. He practised severe austerities such as not eating or drinking and standing upright throughout Lent. From the hut Simeon progressed to the greater solitude of the small ledge of a mountain. But the incessant numbers of pilgrims who came to seek him out compelled him to resort to even sterner measures, and he spent the rest of his life living on the top of a series of four pillars. For the first few years his pillar was a modest nine feet tall, but the next three grew steadily higher – from eighteen feet to thirty-three feet to a vertiginous sixty feet. Perhaps not surprisingly, Simeon's aim to escape the crowds backfired. Pilgrims and curious tourists flocked to see him perched on his eyrie, and talismanic statuettes of the saint and medallions depicting him on his column became popular souvenirs. Those unable to make the journey to his pillar could communicate through letters, which were brought up to him by ladder. Simeon responded to his daily audience by preaching sermons or by ignoring the crowd and carrying on with his customary prayer prostrations, sometimes more than 1,200 a day. He became so famous that even the emperors Theodosius II and Leo came to see him; he also inspired other 'pillar saints' such as Daniel the Stylite (409–93), who lived on a column near Constantinople. When Simeon died in 459 the churches of Antioch and Constantinople vied to possess his remains, with Antioch obtaining the honour. In time, a church and monastery were built in his memory around his column (in modern Qal`at Sim`an in Syria), and their remains continue to draw visitors.

St Jerome and the Holy Land

Other evidence for the popularity of the Holy Land as a destination for pilgrims during the fourth and fifth centuries can be found in the writings of St Jerome (c. 342–420) and the account of a pilgrim named Egeria (also known as Etheria and Sylvia), probably a nun from Spain or southern France, who travelled to the Levant in the early 380s. Although much of Egeria's account has been lost, it is more engaging and informative than that of the Bordeaux Pilgrim. Egeria is constantly enthusiastic about what she does and sees, and she makes careful note of anything relevant to her faith or of practical value to her sister nuns back in the west. She mentions, for example, that during Lent the Jerusalem Christians did not eat oil or anything that grows on trees, 'but only water and a little gruel made from flour'; and that the Greek phrase *Kyrie eleison* ('Lord have mercy') is the equivalent to the Latin *Misere Domine* used at home. She also gives tantalizing glimpses of places outside Palestine such as Mount Sinai, Constantinople and Edessa.

In Jerusalem itself Egeria paid close attention to the order and content of church services and left an invaluable guide to late fourth-century Christian liturgy. She describes the Sunday services at the Church of the Holy Sepulchre, where people gathered in great numbers outside the basilica before dawn, singing hymns and

A Byzantine carving from the fifth or sixth century depicting the hermit St Simeon Stylites atop his pillar being visited by a pilgrim carrying what is probably an incense burner.

antiphons in the lamplit darkness. At the first cockcrow the bishop arrived and the congregation proceeded to the domed rotunda of the Anastasis, where psalms and prayers were recited and censers brought in, filling the interior with fragrance. The bishop then read the narrative of Jesus' resurrection from the New Testament, eliciting weeping and groaning from the congregation. Elsewhere she describes the veneration of the True Cross on Good Friday. The bishop took the sacred wood out of its silver-gilt casket and held it firmly at either end while members of the congregation came up one by one to kiss it – Egeria mentions that a number of deacons stood around the bishop to guard the wood because someone had once tried to bite a piece off it.

A couple of years after Egeria's pilgrimage, St Jerome, best known for his translation of the Bible into the Latin Vulgate text, came to Palestine and settled in Bethlehem, where he spent the rest of his life. Through his authority, writings, and enthusiasm both for the Holy Land and for the cult of the martyrs, Jerome was influential in helping to consolidate the positive attitude of contemporary and later Christians towards the veneration of relics and pilgrimages to sacred places. Jerome was born in Stridon in what is now Slovenia and educated at home and in Rome, where he frequented the catacombs. In about 374 he set off to the east and stayed for a while in Antioch in Syria, where, during an illness, he received a dramatic dream in which he was dragged into a court of the Lord and charged with being more concerned with Cicero – i.e. with pagan literature – than with Christianity. Afterwards he undertook to mend his ways and became a hermit in the deserts of Syria for about five years, where, diverted from his desire for pagan classics, he learned Hebrew, the language of the Old Testament. After his return to Antioch, where he was ordained a priest, he went to Constantinople and then, in 382, he settled in Rome, working as a secretary to Pope Damasus. Three years later he left Rome for Palestine and lived in Bethlehem, where he stayed until his death in 420, running a monastery and a hostel, and studying, teaching and providing hospitality to pilgrims.

Jerome's attitude to the cult of the martyrs can be seen in a letter he wrote attacking a priest named Vigilantius, who had apparently condemned as superstitious customs such as the veneration of relics, vigils in the churches of the martyrs, prayers offered to the dead, and the burning of tapers – criticisms similar to those that would surface more than 1,000 years later during the Reformation (see pages 130–37). In a full-blooded rebuttal, complete with Ciceronian rhetoric, Jerome counteracted Vigilantius' reductive argument that it was absurd to kiss and adore the remains of saints – 'a bit of powder wrapped up in a cloth' – by appealing to authority and tradition. He cited, for example, the occasion when Emperor Arcadius took the bones of the prophet Samuel in procession from Palestine to Constantinople and how the Christians who greeted the relics along the way were 'as joyful as if they had witnessed a living prophet among them'. Jerome accused Vigilantius of lacking imagination

– 'you are sceptical because you think only of the dead body' – and reminded him of the biblical text stating that God is not God of the dead but of the living. In denying the validity of praying to the dead, Vigilantius was denying the whole idea that those in this world were connected with the departed in a relationship of mutual help.

Jerome defended the orthodox view robustly – perhaps more with bombast than logic ('Shall Vigilantius the live dog be better than Paul the dead lion?') – showing the passion and rhetoric that made him enemies and attracted his close band of friends. One of the latter was a widow named Paula, who abandoned her life in Rome to follow him to Bethlehem. In a letter commemorating her some years after her death, Jerome gives a moving account of Paula's piety and her pilgrimages to the holy sites. Paula travelled from Rome by ship, stopping at places that would become familiar in later medieval pilgrim itineraries, such as the islands of Rhodes and Cyprus. When she reached Jerusalem, she displayed a religious fervour and 'concretizing' imagination reminiscent of the medieval English mystic Margery Kempe (see page 125), which Vigilantius would have found abhorrent. 'She threw herself down,' Jerome says, before the True Cross 'as though the Lord was hanging on it'; and in Bethlehem she saw 'with the eyes of faith' the baby Jesus crying in the manger and 'declared she could

ABOVE: St Jerome by the Flemish painter Jan Massys (1508–75). The saint is shown contemplating a skull and holding a copy of his Vulgate translation of the Bible.

see the slaughtered innocents, the raging Herod, Joseph and Mary fleeing into Egypt'. Elsewhere, she visited Hebron, Bethany and the tomb of Lazarus, Jericho, the Jordan and Samaria, where, at certain holy tombs, she witnessed demon-possessed men howling like animals and contorting their bodies, seemingly enraged by the spiritual power of the dead saints.

Paula, along with her daughter Eustochium, settled in Bethlehem, ran a convent of nuns (which Eustochium took over when her mother died in 404) and helped Jerome with his biblical scholarship. Their enthusiasm for the Holy Land comes out in a letter composed in their names by Jerome to a Roman widow named Marcella. In it they plead with her to come and join them in Palestine, arguing that a Christian's spiritual education is incomplete if he or she has not visited Jerusalem. The letter also conjures up a picture of the spiritual power that radiated out from the Holy Land across the empire, drawing pilgrims to Jerusalem from all over the Roman world – including nobles from Gaul and Britons beating a path from the extreme west, as well as Armenians, Persians, Indians, Arabians, Egyptians and others also on the road. The letter ends by trying to tempt Marcella (apparently to no avail) with all the sights she would see if she came; in doing so it gives an interesting list of the pilgrimage places frequented at this period. They include: Nazareth, where Jesus grew up; Cana, where he turned water into wine; Mount Tabor, where he was transfigured into a radiant figure of light; the spot in Galilee where he fed the multitude with a few loaves and fishes; the town of Nain, where he brought to life the dead son of a widow; Capernaum, which he used as his base during his ministry in Galilee. There was also the River Jordan and the Mount of Olives – scenes of Jesus' baptism and Passion – and, of course, his tomb. In centuries to come, this pilgrimage trail would be augmented by the joint grave of Paula and Eustochium themselves. It lay, according to the record of a twelfth-century Anglo-Saxon or German pilgrim named Saewulf, beneath the southern altar of the church in Bethlehem.

Jerusalem, from one of the greatest early maps of biblical lands, the Madaba Mosaic in Jordan (c. 560). The beginning of the city's name can be seen in the Greek letters IEPOYCA at the top.

DARK AGE JOURNEYS

'My voice sticks in my throat; and as I dictate, sobs choke my words.' So wrote St Jerome in 410 as he remembered the recent sack of Rome by the Visigoths, one of the more notable landmarks in the protracted decline and fall of the Western Roman Empire. News of the capture of the Eternal City reached Jerome in far-off Palestine and, in a letter to a woman named Principia, he described the shock of hearing that the 'city which had conquered the world was itself conquered'.

Hypotheses as to why the Roman Empire fell in the West are as numerous as the barbarian tribes who swarmed over the imperial borders in the fifth century AD. It has been proposed that the growth of Christianity and its pacifist ideology neutered Rome's belligerent instincts, or that the fundamental problem lay in the weakness of central government or in the decline of urban life and a downward economic spiral coupled with a punitive tax system. Unfavourable climatic conditions and epidemics of plague have also been mooted. The truth may be that all these factors played a part, and that it is too difficult to disentangle which were causes and which effects. In any case, the immediate beneficiaries of Rome's ills were the barbarian tribes – the Germanic peoples who had been living around the fringes of the empire, casting envious glances at its relative prosperity and peace. In the late fourth century, Emperor Theodosius I had tried to negate the threat of the Goths and other tribes by permitting them to live inside the empire and giving them the status of *foederati*, or allies. But even this desperate measure failed to stem the advance of yet more Germans, themselves harried by the movement of aggressive Central Asian tribes and eager for the decaying but still attractive fruits of the empire. Franks, Ostrogoths, Saxons, Angles, Alans, Burgundians and others penetrated almost all parts of the Western Empire as well as North Africa, where the Vandals established a kingdom. In 476 the last Western Roman emperor, Romulus Augustus, was deposed by the German leader of the Roman Army, itself a hotchpotch of barbarian mercenaries.

By the beginning of the 500s, Germanic tribes had established kingdoms within the borders of the old empire, thus inaugurating the so-called Dark Ages – though these centuries were not without light. The structures of imperial civilization lingered on, albeit in diminished forms, and managed to inspire admiration and imitation among the new conquerors. Barbarian nobles called themselves by Roman titles and copied

Roman manners and customs. They married Roman women, learned to speak and write Latin, and many were already Christian, if only of the heretical Arian variety. The Ostrogothic king Theodoric, who ruled Italy from 493 to 526, repaired the infrastructure of his domains and patronized the arts. In Gaul, Clovis, king of the Franks, established a strong government and in 496 converted to Catholic Christianity. He and his successors (known as the Merovingians after a Frankish ancestor named Merovech) laid the foundations of Frankish power, which reached a glorious climax in the figure of Charlemagne (768–814).

A Light in the West

The Church, with its learning and clear lines of authority, still underpinned what remained of civilization on continental Europe during the fifth century. But the situation farther west, in Britain and Ireland, was different. The pagan Angles, Saxons and Jutes invaded Britain and remorselessly wore down the Romano-British population, eventually establishing kingdoms in almost the entire country except the far west. In Ireland, too remote for the German tribes – as it had been for the Roman legions – the people continued their distinctive Celtic pagan way of life undisturbed. The Irish worshipped a number of gods, and their religious rites were ordered by a powerful priestly caste known as the Druids. Society revolved around the courts of numerous petty kings – nominally owing allegiance to a high king – who fought among themselves and launched piratical raids on the west coast of Britain for slaves and other booty.

Yet in a relatively short period of time, Ireland, and a little later Britain, was to produce a stream of Christian saints and scholars, learned and burning with religious ardour, who sailed across to Europe as missionaries, monks, hermits, teachers and pilgrims. There they founded monasteries, churches and hostels, spread the word of God among the pagans and semi-pagans, and strengthened the faith of their fellow Christians. How did this phenomenon come about? Although the Irish would have come into contact with Christianity through trading connections and the capture of British slaves, it was not until 431 that Pope Celestine sent a certain Palladius to be Ireland's first bishop. How much Palladius achieved is debatable; and whatever he did do was cast in the shade by St Patrick (*c.* 390–460). A Briton by birth, Patrick was

seized by Irish pirates when he was sixteen years old and taken off to be a slave in the country he would later convert. After six years of slavery he escaped and eventually returned home, but a vision-like dream convinced him to return to Ireland as a Christian missionary. He spent the rest of his life travelling around the country, spreading the Gospel, converting local chieftains, ordaining priests and laying solid foundations for the growth of the Irish Church. In the century following his death, great monasteries arose in Clonard, Clonmacnoise, Derry, Durrow, Bangor and elsewhere, and Irish monks began to give up the security of home to set out abroad in search of new opportunities – usually in isolated and dangerous places – to fulfil their spiritual vocations. Some would set sail to remote islands, 'deserts in the ocean' as they were known, such as the Orkneys; or they would set up hermitages in inhospitable regions in Britain or Europe. Some founded great monasteries, such as Luxeuil in France or St. Gall in Switzerland. The word used to refer to these wandering Irish monks was *peregrinus*, which meant at first simply 'foreigner' but came to signify 'pilgrim', though in some cases it is not clear which sense is meant. In fact some early Irish *peregrini* were convicted criminals who had been sentenced to wander abroad as exiles, sometimes forever. But the term is most usually associated with the saints and monks who for several centuries set off of their own accord into the unknown, letting God guide their footsteps or sails.

The *peregrinatio* – this practice of wandering without a fixed destination, for the love of God – was a variant on traditional goal-directed pilgrimage. Although part of the purpose of the Irish *peregrini* was to live as hermits or as missionaries, they also actively sought out the experience of later medieval pilgrims: long, lonely journeys, physical hardship and danger, and the chance to visit and pray in holy places. What made these early Irish pilgrims different from later medieval ones was the fact that they did not have a predetermined destination and that they were prepared, having set out, never to see their homeland again. They simply trusted God to show them the way. A good example of this attitude can be found in the early medieval historical record known as the *Anglo-Saxon Chronicle*, which tells how one day in 891 three

The monastery of Clonmacnoise in County Offaly, Ireland, founded by
St Ciaran in 545, was to become a major European centre of scholarship.

Irishmen landed on the coast of Cornwall in a boat that had no oars. The men said that they wanted to 'live in a state of pilgrimage, for the love of God, they cared not where'. They had taken provisions for just seven days and had reached Cornwall just before their food ran out.

St Brendan the Navigator

One of the great inspirational figures of these early Irish *peregrini* was Brendan of Clonfert (*c.* 486–578), known as the Navigator. Brendan's legendary voyage to the west in search of the 'Island Promised to the Saints' is recounted in the tenth-century *Navigatio Sancti Brendani*, a medieval Latin best-seller that was translated into French, Breton, Flemish, Welsh and many other languages. In the story Brendan sets sail from southwest Ireland with seventeen fellow monks on a voyage lasting seven years. After the first forty days they arrive at the first of many islands and witness the first of many miracles: they are guided by a benevolent dog to a mysterious hall where they find jugs of water and then fish and bread laid out for them. They reach their next island on Maundy Thursday and encounter sheep the 'size of bulls'. Then a man suddenly appears who acts as their spiritual guide or steward. He informs the monks that they will spend the night of the coming Easter vigil on an unnamed nearby island, but Easter Sunday itself on one called the Paradise of Birds. The monks duly reach the neighbouring island; but when they come to light a fire to cook their food, the island – it is in fact a whale – starts to move, prompting them to scramble for their boat and make off in great haste.

On the Paradise of Birds, they find a tree filled with pure white birds who can speak and sing psalms, and who turn out to be fallen angels. One of them tells Brendan that in the following years he and his men will keep returning to the same islands to celebrate Easter before eventually reaching their desired destination. And so it proves. The voyage continues in its inexorable circular rhythm, punctuated by surreal sights and dangerous encounters. The monks witness, for example, a fire-breathing creature destroying a sea monster; they come to an island where three choirs – of boys, youths and men, dressed in white, blue and purple robes respectively – are singing psalms; they are brought grapes the size of apples by a bird that saves them from a menacing griffin; they sail past a huge column of pure crystal rising from the sea; they approach the grim smoking mountain of hell; and they come across a man perched on a rock out at sea – it turns out to be Judas, who has been granted the temporary respite of the rock from the torments of hell.

Towards the end of their voyage, the monks arrive at an island where they discover the amazing 140-year-old, Robinson Crusoe-like figure of Paul the Hermit, whose naked body is bristling all over with snow-white hair. Paul recognizes Brendan as someone specially favoured by God – a propitious omen as the voyage, and the story, draws to an end. After a final Easter spent on their now-familiar islands, the monks are guided by the good steward to the Island Promised to the Saints. Negotiating a dark fog, they reach the shore and find the island full of fruit trees. They venture forth inland for forty days and finally come to a river where a young man suddenly appears, blesses them and says that they have found their destination and now must return home. So, abruptly and without more ado, they set off back to Ireland, laden with fruit and jewels, to receive a rapturous welcome from the brethren of Clonfert.

Whether Brendan actually made the voyage described in the *Navigatio*, or something like it, is still debated. During his life the saint was renowned as a traveller at least around the British Isles and possibly Britanny. Mixed in with the *Navigatio*'s miraculous happenings are nuggets of practical information suggestive of an actual voyage. Brendan's boat, we are told, consisted of a tanned oxhide stretched over a ribbed wooden frame; seams were greased with animal fat; propulsion was by sail and oars; and spare animal skins and extra fat were stored on board. In 1976 the British explorer Tim Severin decided to see whether Brendan's voyage would have been possible with early medieval materials and technology. Building a wooden-framed, oxhide boat, he set out from Ireland to America, via the Faroes, Iceland and Greenland. Severin's epic trip was a startling success. His boat, the *Brendan*, reached the New World, surviving salt-water attrition, stormy seas and ice floes. Severin also suggested identifications between some of the *Navigatio*'s descriptions and landmarks on his own voyage: the island of giant sheep with the Faroes, where sheep abound; the mountain of hell with the southern volcanic region of Iceland; the column of crystal with the icebergs off Greenland; and the fog-bound but ultimately fruitful Island Promised to the Saints with Newfoundland. The islands in the *Navigatio* inhabited by monks and hermits might also reflect the fact that Irish monks did actually settle in remote places such as the Hebrides, the Faroes and Iceland. Also, the Brendan of the story resembles actual *peregrini* in the way he is prepared to entrust his vessel to God, as when he tells his men: 'The Lord is our captain and helmsman, is he not? Then let Him direct us where He wills.'

Severin's experiences showed that it is possible the *Navigatio* drew on an actual voyage or on descriptive elements of a number of voyages. Yet for all its authentic sea lore, the *Navigatio* is also pervaded with an atmosphere of the supernatural, a characteristic of the medieval *Lives* of saints, which mix fact with legend. In addition, the *Navigatio* draws on a rich tradition of pagan Irish stories of 'adventures' (*echtrai*) and 'voyages' (*immrama*), which are also filled with the miraculous. Examples include the 'Voyage of Bran', in which the eponymous hero sets out to find the Land of Women; and the 'Voyage of Maeldúin', in which Maeldúin, searching for his father's killer, lands on thirty-one islands, where he finds, *inter alia*, giant ants, weeping mourners, shouting birds and a great arc of water.

Apart from its stream of miracles, there are other elements that give the *Navigatio* an air of unreality, such as the recurring symbolism of the numbers three and forty, with their biblical connotations of the Trinity, the three days of Easter and the forty days of Lent. There is also a marked emphasis on religious observance – celebrating Mass, singing psalms – which gives the story a strong sacramental character and the sense of a liturgical rhythm in harmony with the circular rhythm of the voyage. And although Brendan resembles actual *peregrini* in some ways, he differs from them in one crucial aspect – the fact that he has a clear goal: the Island Promised to the Saints. It is this that gives the *Navigatio* its strong narrative current and sense of mission. Like Jason and the Argonauts, or Odysseus, or the heroes of the Irish *immrama*, Brendan has a specific destination in mind. This factor also make the dangers the monks encounter seem purposeful, as if their faith and mettle must be tested before they can reach their goal, their promised land. When they do eventually arrive, the young man who greets them says that the Lord did not let them find the island straightaway

A plate from the *Navigatio Sancti Brendani*. Brendan and his companions make ready to sail off from an 'island' that they discover to be a whale (named Jasconius) after lighting a fire on its back.

because he wanted to show them the rich wonders of the ocean. But these 'wonders' have included monsters, the marooned Judas and a vision of a volcanic hell. The wonders seem to have a moral purpose: together they give the sense of a progressive spiritual initiation, a pilgrimage of the soul. By fusing echoes of an actual voyage with that of a spiritual journey the *Navigatio* straddles two worlds, one of Atlantic voyaging with echoes of the historical *peregrinatio*, the other of internal spiritual journeying.

COLUMBANUS AND OTHER SAINTS

If Brendan is the archetypal Irish *peregrinus* of the sea, his counterpart on land is arguably St Columbanus (*c.* 543–615), a passionate, dynamic monk of great determination, with a penchant for extreme asceticism. Columbanus founded the important monasteries of Annegray and Luxeuil in Burgundy, and Bobbio in Italy, wrote an influential monastic rule and set an example to posterity as a fearless moralist and missionary. He referred to himself as a *peregrinus* and, according to his contemporary biographer Jonas, he took as his guiding light the words God spoke to Abraham in Genesis 12:1: 'Leave your country, your people and your father's household and go to a land I will show you.' He was essentially a free spirit, acutely aware of the fleeting nature of life on earth, and prepared to abandon security and comfort for the hardship his questing soul demanded. His whole life, with its long, hazardous physical journeys, and spiritual peaks and troughs, reads like the arduous pilgrimage he believed a Christian's destiny to be. Columbanus was born in Leinster in Ireland. After a number of years at the monastery of Bangor, he decided to become 'an exile for the sake of Christ'. So in about 590 he sailed off with a group of twelve companions to the coast of Brittany and made his way inland to Frankish Gaul. The monks' first settlement was in Burgundy where the local king Guntram allowed them to found a monastery on the site of a ruined castle in Annegray, in the wilds of the Vosges. There they subsisted on tree bark, roots and herbs, and the charitable offerings of local people. Before long, Columbanus gained a reputation for holiness and began to attract visitors seeking cures for illnesses. More monks joined the ranks of the original twelve, and soon Columbanus decided he needed a larger monastery, which he proceeded to found about eight miles away at a place called Luxeuil. But as the flow of visitors and recruits continued unabated, the saint established yet another house in nearby Fontaine. He then alternated between Luxeuil and Fontaine, organizing the daily lives of his monks along the lines of his monastic rule. Jonas reports that he also worked miracles and communicated with animals. These included a pet squirrel he would call down from the tree tops and carry on his neck, and a bear he ordered away from a dead stag, explaining to it that the hide was needed for shoes.

The harmonious life Columbanus established in his monasteries did not last. The saint fell foul of the latest Frankish king of Burgundy, Theoderic, and his powerful scheming grandmother Brunhild; and it was no help that the local Frankish bishops, piqued by the Irishman's irregular lifestyle and criticism of their worldliness, viewed him with disfavour. In short, Columbanus and his Irish brethren were commanded to leave Luxeuil and go back to Ireland. With great reluctance, Columbanus eventually complied with the order and set out homewards with his monks on another long 'pilgrimage', as he called it. They made their way to Auxerre and Nevers, then proceeded by boat along the Loire to Orléans and Tours, where Columbanus spent the whole night in prayer at the grave of St Martin. They finally reached Nantes at the head of the Loire estuary, where they intended to embark for Ireland. Destiny decreed otherwise, however. As soon as the ship bearing the monks and their possessions set sail, a huge wave drove it back to the shore, where it remained, unable to move, for three days. But when the captain offloaded 'all that belonged to Columbanus', a wave washed the ship out to sea and, Jonas concluded, 'all, filled with amazement, understood that God did not wish Columbanus to return home'. Instead, Columbanus decided he would make his home in Italy, and managed to enlist the help of Chlotar, king of the Western Franks, who provided an armed escort for the journey. So again the monks set off for a new life, progressing by way of Paris, Meaux, Ussy and Metz on the River Moselle, along the Rhine to Mainz, then on to Bregenz on Lake Constance. There he stayed for a while, preaching the Gospel to the local pagan Slavic tribes. But this was not to be his final destination. One day he received a vision of an angel who showed him 'in a little circle the structure of the world, just as the circle of the universe is usually drawn with a pen in a book'. The angel pointed out how much of the world had yet to hear the word of God and that, whatever the direction in which Columbanus travelled, his missionary endeavours would be rewarded.

Once more Columbanus set off, this time to northern Italy. He left behind his companion Gall, who went on to Christianize Switzerland, giving his name to the town of St Gall and the renowned monastery he founded there. In Italy, welcomed by Agilulf, king of the Lombards, Columbanus settled at a fertile spot in the Apennines called Bobbio (the name of a local stream, abounding with fish) where he found a ruined church. Now in his early seventies, Columbanus set about rebuilding the dilapidated building with his customary vigour, carrying tree trunks, Jonas says, with the strength of thirty men. Bobbio was the end of Columbanus' pilgrimage. In 615, within a year or so of his arrival, he died on 21 November, the date of his feast day.

Columbanus was a giant among the early Irish *peregrini* and one of the first to journey from Ireland for the sake of Christ. But there were many others who followed his example. The seventh-century Irish monk Fiacra, for example, established a hermitage in northern France in Breuil, east of Paris. Near to his solitary dwelling he built a hostel for pilgrims and travellers, and after his death his grave became a destination for pilgrims. As a result of his prowess at growing vegetables, medicinal herbs and other plants he became the patron saint of horticulturists. His contemporary Kilian made his way to Germany, sailing along the Rhine and the Main to Würzburg, where he converted the local pagan ruler Gozbert. He was later supposed to have been murdered at the instigation of Gozbert's wife, enraged that Kilian had dared to pronounce her marriage invalid since she was the widow of Gozbert's brother.

One of the best recorded lives of this period is that of St Fursey, who, according to the eighth-century English monk and historian Bede, vowed to 'spend his life as a pilgrim for love of our Lord and to go wherever God should call him'. In about 633 he left Ireland, sailed to Britain and founded a monastery in East Anglia. Then in 648 he made his way to Gaul with a small band of companions, and founded a monastery in Lagny-sur-Marne near Paris. He died two years later and was laid to rest at Péronne in Picardy, where for thirty days pilgrims came to pay their respects to his mortal remains, which they found 'incorrupt and exhaling a sweet odour'. Fursey was also famous for receiving a vision of the afterlife which included a glimpse of hell that was said to have left him with physical scorch marks.

If the Irish led the way as pilgrims and missionaries in the wildernesses of western

Europe, the English were not far behind them. The conversion of Anglo-Saxon England to Christianity was due at first to the work of Irish missionaries working mainly in the north. Then in 597 a group of thirty Roman monks, under their leader Augustine, landed in Kent with orders from Pope Gregory I to evangelize the country. By 601 King Ethelbert of Kent had converted to the faith, and soon English-born monks were spreading the word of God among their pagan kinsmen. By the end of the seventh century, the orthodox Roman faith they preached had eclipsed the Celtic Christianity of the Irish, who differed in their dating of Easter and in the style of their monastic tonsures. Before long English *peregrini*, like their Irish counterparts, were heading off to the continent, travelling to secluded spots to practise the life of the spirit, strengthen the faith of their fellow Christians and bring the word of God to the pagans.

One such questing English monk was Willibrord, a Yorkshireman who spent twelve years as a pilgrim in Ireland before setting off, in 690, to Frisia. There he was given support for his endeavours by the Frankish king Pippin II and Pope Sergius, who made him Archbishop of Utrecht. An august, enthusiastic figure, Willibrord founded new monasteries and churches, and undermined the local pagans by destroying their sacred cult objects. At the time of his death he had succeeded in laying the basis of Christianity in the region. Farther east, in Germany, Willibrord's younger contemporary St Boniface, possibly from Crediton in Devon, achieved even more substantial results for the Faith. Arguably his most famous act was cutting down a sacred pagan oak tree at Geismar, in east-central Germany: because the gods seemingly allowed this sacrilege to occur without wreaking vengeance large numbers of pagans instantly converted. Boniface was eventually made Archbishop of Mainz and in this position he was able to create bishops, found monasteries and generally strengthen the Frankish Church.

One of the weaknesses of the pagan Anglo-Saxon religion had been its absence of an afterlife. Bede memorably describes how one of the councillors of the pagan king Edwin of Northumbria likened life to a sparrow that flies in and out of a banqueting hall, experiencing a little bit of light and warmth before returning to the darkness from which it came. That was the best a pagan could hope for. Christianity, with its system of heaven, hell and purgatory, added a new, post-mortem dimension, but one which had its own sources of anxiety (see pages 62–66). Partly in response to this, pilgrimage became popular at all levels of society. In the late 680s Caedwalla, the king of Wessex, abdicated his throne in order to make the journey to Rome in the hope of being baptized at 'the shrine of the blessed Apostles' and then ending his days shortly afterwards in this blessed state. The king arrived in 688, received baptism then promptly fell ill and died still wearing his white baptismal clothing. After thirty-seven years of power, Ine, Caedwalla's successor, also abdicated his throne and trekked to Rome, hoping that his visit to the sacred city would gain him a benevolent reception by the saints when he died. Bede reports that many followed the example of these two kings: 'nobles and peasants, lay people and clerics, men and women'.

Pilgrimage was popular among the English also at a local level. One well known

shrine was that of St Chad, whom Aidan, the Irish bishop of Lindisfarne, had sent to Ireland to deepen his knowledge of the Faith. After Chad's death in 672 at Lichfield in central England, his body was placed in a tomb shaped like a small wooden house, with a hole in one side to allow pilgrims to stretch through and gather dust made holy by its proximity to the saint. Bede records that a convent in Barking in Essex attracted the sick, and he cites the case of a blind woman who regained her sight by praying before relics of the saints in the convent's burial ground. He also recorded that the relics of St Cuthbert of Lindisfarne, who died in 687, effected miraculous cures. A paralysed monk named Badudegn felt the sensation of a 'large, broad hand' easing the pain in his body; and a monk at a monastery in Penrith, who had a tumour on his eyelid, was healed after he applied a few of Cuthbert's hairs taken from his shrine.

During the sixth and seventh centuries, then, Irish *peregrini*, as well as their English counterparts, were heading off to Europe as 'Christ's exiles'. By the 700s, however, the initial vigour of this movement had begun to wane and Christians on the continent were viewing the *peregrini* more critically. As the Church became better organized and the monastic rule of St Benedict was established throughout the Carolingian Empire, tolerance diminished for these wandering, less accountable pilgrims. As historian Kathleen Hughes has written: 'The traditional idea of Irish pilgrimage could no longer be accommodated in the climate of Benedictine stability.' Although in the 800s Irish pilgrims were still crossing the seas to Gaul, they were more likely to be making conventional pilgrimages to Rome or serving as scholars in Carolingian monasteries. At the same time monastic reformers in Ireland, eager to exert more discipline on their brethren, were encouraging them not to leave their homeland. Expressive of these new attitudes is an anonymous contemporary Irish poem that declared: 'There is a heavy toll/Involved in journeying to Rome/And very little gain./The king you wish to find in Rome/You'll seek and seek in vain/Unless he travels in your soul.'

A tenth-century German illuminated manuscript showing the martyrdom of St Boniface at Dokkum in Frisia in 754. The evangelical travels of Boniface brought about the baptism of many Germans (illustrated to the right of the column).

DECLINE AND REVIVAL

In the seventh and eighth centuries, while Irish and English *peregrini* were travelling to northern Europe, the Church in the Mediterranean world was reeling from the onslaught of a militant new religion: Islam. The rise and spread of Islam was sudden and devastating. Founded by the Prophet Muhammad, who died in 632, the Muslim faith fanned out rapidly from its heartland of Arabia. By this time, the two major powers of the region, the Christian Byzantine Empire and Persia had worn each other out in constant warfare like two heavyweight boxers. The conditions were ripe for the fast-moving, disciplined and zealous Arab cavalry to inflict defeat after defeat on their enemies. Within decades of the Prophet's death Muslim armies had swept eastwards into Iran, north into Palestine (Jerusalem fell in 638), Syria and eastern Turkey, and westwards along the North African coast to what is now Morocco. Then in 711 a Muslim Arab and Berber army from North Africa crossed the Strait of Gibraltar and invaded Christian Visigothic Spain, conquering most of it in seven years. By 720 they had pushed into France, making headway as far as the Loire. They were finally halted at Poitiers in 732 by the Franks under Charles Martel.

Although defeat at Poitiers balked the Muslim advance into northern Europe for good, Muslim rule now extended from the Atlantic to the borders of India and included many of Christianity's most holy places. How did this affect pilgrim traffic to the Holy Land? There is evidence that after the initial fall of Jerusalem many pilgrims preferred Rome as a destination. In time, however, the Holy Land regained much of its popularity. For on the whole, Muslim rulers adopted a relatively tolerant attitude to the Jews and Christians under their control, allowing them to practise their religion so long as they paid a poll tax. Also, since the pilgrimage to Mecca was one of the 'five pillars' of Islam, Muslims could at least understand the motives of Christian pilgrims. A Gallic monk named Bernard who made the pilgrimage to Jerusalem in about 870 said that relations between Christians and Muslims were excellent – so long as the Christians had their permits in order.

At a later period, in the eleventh century, a more militant Muslim regime hindered access to the holy places, prompting the Crusades (see pages 59–60). Until then it seems that Western pilgrims, armed with passes and money for tips and bribes, were able to visit Palestine without too much difficulty. Two such pilgrims of the seventh and eighth centuries were a bishop of Gaul named Arculf and an English monk named Willibald, the only Englishman of this period known to have recorded his pilgrimage. Arculf went to Jerusalem in the 680s and later, during a stay at the monastery of Iona (see pages 169–74), he described his journey to the abbot Adomnan, biographer of St Columba. In Jerusalem Arculf visited the Church of the Holy Sepulchre and was especially impressed by the domed Anastasis that enclosed the cavern-like tomb chamber of the Lord. He also saw various holy relics and sites, including the lance that pierced Jesus' side and his burial shroud, the fig tree from which Judas hanged himself and the Mount of Olives, from where Jesus ascended into heaven. The actual spot of the Ascension was marked by a round roofless church – roofless so that pilgrims could trace the path taken by the Lord. Arculf visited this church often and reported that Jesus' last footprints were visible in the earth, even though pilgrims were allowed to stretch through the protective railings to gather bits of holy dust.

About forty years after Arculf's visit Willibald set out on a pilgrimage to Rome and the Holy Land. Having stayed in Rome for more than two years, he sailed off to Palestine by way of Sicily, the tip of the Greek Peloponnese, the islands of Chios and Samos, the city of Ephesus and Cyprus. In Palestine Willibald and his party were immediately arrested by the 'Saracens' – as Westerners called the Muslims – on suspicion of spying. They were released on payment of a ransom and travelled south via Damascus to Jerusalem. There Willibald, too, visited the Church of the Holy Sepulchre. He mentioned seeing three wooden crosses placed outside the eastern end of the church to commemorate the crucifixion; on entering Jesus' tomb chamber he was struck by the sight of fifteen oil-filled golden bowls, placed on a shelf, which burned night and day. Like Arculf, Willibald visited the Church of the Ascension on the Mount of Olives, but did not remark on the 'Lord's footprints'. What he saw instead was a constantly burning lantern placed at the centre of the church. He also noted the local tradition that anyone who could squeeze through the narrow space between the columns and the walls would be freed from his or her sins. In all, Willibald spent two to three years in the Holy Land, visiting sacred sites and recovering from bouts of sickness. When he eventually left in about 726 he successfully smuggled a large pot of precious balsam past the Muslim customs officials

– an enormous risk since had it been discovered he would apparently have been put to death. Willibald sailed back westwards via Constantinople, Sicily and a small, unnamed volcanic island to the north, where he watched flames belching from the crater and plumes of smoke jetting upwards to the sky. But he never returned to England. After a period at the monastery of Monte Cassino near Naples, he was sent to Germany by Pope Gregory III, where he became bishop of Eichstätt and founded the 'double' monastery (for men and women) of Heidenheim.

By the time Willibald died in 786, most of western Christendom was under the sway of Charlemagne (768–814), the greatest of the Frankish kings, who was crowned Holy Roman Emperor in 800. During his forty-six-year rule, he expanded his territories, spread and strengthened the Christian faith, and encouraged culture and learning. At his court in Aachen he gathered the leading scholars and teachers of the time, including Peter of Pisa, Paul the Deacon and, especially, Alcuin of York; and he made sure that monks throughout the empire were engaged in transcribing the works of the classical authors. He overhauled the administration of his empire, standardized laws and improved the discipline of the Church, imposing unity on liturgical practices. He also ameliorated conditions for missionaries and pilgrims. In 802 a decree stated that pilgrims must not be denied shelter or water, and in 813 the Council of Tours declared that bishops must give hospitality to the poor and to pilgrims. His good diplomatic relationship with the Muslim caliph Harun ar-Rashid (786–809) led to his building a hostel for pilgrims in Jerusalem. When the Gallic monk Bernard visited the city in about 870 he reaped the rewards of the emperor's enlightened policy when he stayed at this hostel, 'of the Most Glorious Emperor Charles', which was open to all pilgrims who spoke Latin. At the church next door Bernard was delighted to find that Charlemagne had endowed it with a 'magnificent library'.

Bernard's chronicle of his pilgrimage is the last detailed account of a pilgrimage before the period of the Crusades. Setting out from Rome in about 870, Bernard travelled eastwards across Italy to Mount Gargano, then south to Bari – at that time

Charlemagne succeeded in uniting a large swathe of Christian Europe
politically and culturally under the Frankish empire. The church at his
capital in Aachen houses this fourteenth-century reliquary bust.

under Muslim control – and Taranto, at the top of Italy's heel. From there he and his companions set sail for Alexandria. In Egypt they made their way by river to Tanis, in the Eastern Delta, and from there to Farama, where the desert stretched away before them 'completely white like a landscape covered in snow'. From Farama Bernard headed north, presumably by camel, to Gaza and then eventually to Jerusalem. There Bernard witnessed the 'ceremony of the Holy Fire' – the first recorded account of the practice, which still continues – at the Church of the Holy Sepulchre on Easter Saturday. As the congregation sang the *Kyrie eleison* during the morning service, 'an angel' supposedly appeared and lit the lamps hanging above Jesus' sepulchre. From these the patriarch of Jerusalem lit a taper and passed the flame on to the lamps of the bishops, who in turn lit those of the ordinary people, so that the whole church blazed with light. Elsewhere in Jerusalem Bernard was shown a number of holy sites, including St Simeon's Church on Mount Sion, where Jesus 'washed the feet of his disciples'; the church 'where we are told St Mary died'; a church that marked the spot of St Stephen's martyrdom; and a church that commemorated Peter's threefold denial of Christ. As for the Muslims' Dome of the Rock, the most visible 'wonder' of Jerusalem, Bernard lists it merely as a 'Saracen synagogue'.

After stopping off at Bethlehem and the Jordan, Bernard set sail from Joppa back to Italy and Rome. There he and his party visited the churches of St John Lateran and St Peter's, and Bernard noted that 'innumerable bodies of saints lie buried in this city'. He continued his pilgrimage through France and ended it, as far as is recorded, at Mont-Saint-Michel, a small rocky islet off the coast near Saint-Malo, connected to the mainland at low tide by a causeway. The Mont's sacred tradition goes back to the early 700s when St Aubert founded an oratory there. Bernard reports that in his day there was a church dedicated to St Michael. In 966 a Benedictine monastery was built, establishing the Mont as an important pilgrim destination in later medieval times.

THE VIKING ERA

While the journey to Jerusalem was still relatively viable for Christians from the eighth to the tenth centuries, holy places and their pilgrimages throughout much of western Europe suffered greatly as a result of raids and invasions by Vikings from Scandinavia. The Viking era of military expansion and settlement began at the end of the 700s and lasted for more than 200 years. Driven by a shortage of good land at home and the lure of easy pickings abroad, pagan warriors from Denmark, Norway and Sweden set sail in their longships – picturesquely dubbed by Viking poets 'surf dragons', 'oar steeds' and 'fjord elks' – to plunder Britain, Ireland, France, Italy and other parts of Europe. In 793 the monastery of Lindisfarne was burnt, and within several years longships were landing on the shores of Ireland. Continental Europe fared better for a while, probably because of the strength of Charlemagne's empire. But after the emperor's death in 814 Viking aggression increased. In 834 the 'Northmen' raided Frisia; in 836 they sacked Antwerp; five years later, Rouen was burnt; the following year it was the turn of Nantes. In 845 the Vikings attacked Paris and were paid 7,000 pounds of silver to leave and not come back – a delaying tactic also used by the English, who called their protection money 'Danegeld'. A contemporary Frankish monk named Ermentarius wrote that 'the unstoppable flow of Vikings never stops increasing. Christians are massacred, burnt and plundered everywhere – the undeniable evidence for which will last until the end of the world.' In 860 a Viking fleet penetrated the western Mediterranean and sacked Pisa and Luna in Italy. Four years later 'a great heathen host', as the *Anglo-Saxon Chronicle* described it, arrived in England, ominously intent on a prolonged invasion, not a swift raid.

Viking expansion in England came to a halt only with the rise of Alfred the Great of Wessex (871–99), who eventually defeated the Danes and forced them to live behind a fixed boundary. Across the Channel in France, in 911 the Frankish king Charles the Simple granted the Norwegian Vikings under Rollo lands in the northwest, hoping they would settle down and act as a bulwark against further incursions by their kinsmen. In time these Northmen gave their name to the region – Normandy – and their descendants became

The terrifying figurehead from an eighth-century Viking longship. The advanced design of Viking ships gave them the speed and manoeuvreability to make sudden attacks on areas across Europe.

a formidable power in their own right.

At about the same time as Rollo and his fellow Vikings were acclimatizing to life as permanent settlers, Europe was disrupted by other raiders. In the east, the Magyars, a semi-nomadic people from the Asian steppes, launched attacks on eastern France, southern Germany and northern Italy, while in the western Mediterranean Muslim pirates ambushed Christian ships. Eventually, however, the turmoil of the tenth century eased. In 955 the German king Otto I defeated the Magyars decisively at the River Lech near Augsburg; and in the 970s a French force neutralized the Muslim pirates. With the aggression of the Vikings now mostly spent, Europe could breathe a small sigh of relief. The morale of the Church also began to revive through the immensely influential monastery of Cluny in Burgundy.

Founded in 910 in an area untouched by Viking incursions and near a major pilgrim road to Rome, Cluny prospered under its first abbots, especially St Odo (927–42). He presided over monastic reforms – based on a stricter interpretation of the Benedictine rule – both at Cluny and its ever-increasing number of sister houses in France, Germany, England, Spain and elsewhere. The Cluniacs put greater emphasis than before on the liturgy and less on manual labour. They ensured that their abbots and priors were freely elected, accountable only to the Pope, and not subject to secular control. Cluny was also the leading light in the 'Peace of God' movement, formulated in 989 at a council in Burgundy. At this it was declared that anyone who attacked a member of the clergy or a church or who stole from a peasant would be excommunicated. The list of potential victims was later extended to include women, children and pilgrims. Further councils throughout the eleventh century continued to assert that pilgrims and other groups should not be molested but enjoy 'perpetual peace'. Cluny also served pilgrims in other ways, notably by building hospices, hostels and bridges on pilgrim roads to Santiago de Compostela (see pages 99–104).

The town of Cluny in Burgundy. In the centre is visible the tower of the abbey's south transept. This imposing Romanesque structure is all that remains of the vast and influential abbey that assisted the development of pilgrimage across Europe.

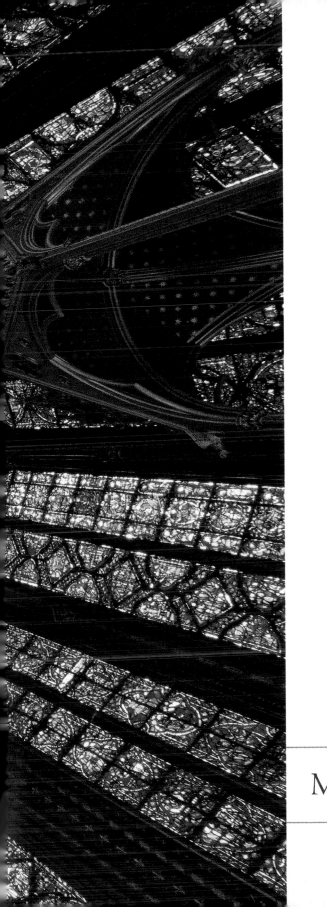

MEDIEVAL ROADS

THE NEW MILLENNIUM

A few years after the start of the second millennium, a Cluniac monk named Ralph Glaber noted that Italy, France and other parts of Europe seemed to be celebrating the fact that the world had not come to an end – as had been feared by many Christians – by renovating and building churches, vying with each other to construct the grandest. 'It was as if the whole earth,' Glaber wrote, 'having cast off the old by shaking itself, were clothing itself everywhere in a white cloak of churches.' His words conveniently sum up the optimistic spirit of this new era. Europe had recovered from the batterings of the Vikings, Magyars and Muslims, and now almost the entire continent was Christian apart from the Baltic lands and areas of Spain and Sicily, where the Muslims still held sway. By the second half of the century towns and cities were beginning to expand significantly and to glorify God with ambitious building projects. King Edward the Confessor (1003–66) had Westminster Abbey rebuilt, in Venice St Mark's was refashioned in the shape of a Greek cross and in 1031 and 1070 cathedrals were consecrated in Strasbourg and Lucca respectively. Santiago de Compostela was attracting more pilgrims, whose journeys were helped by the construction of bridges and hospices along the way. New places of pilgrimage sprang up, such as the Burgundian abbey of Vézelay, which in about 1040 proclaimed that it possessed the body of Mary Magdalene; and Salerno, where from 1080 onwards the body of St Matthew could be visited.

The pilgrimage to the Holy Land also remained popular, even though the land was controlled by the Muslims and subject to the whim of their rulers. The capricious caliph al-Hakim (996–1021), for example, destroyed the Church of the Holy Sepulchre in Jerusalem and persecuted Christians. Then after his death succeeding caliphs restored the status quo and pilgrims resumed their journeys in even greater numbers – Glaber noted that the tomb of Jesus was visited by 'an innumerable multitude' from all over the world, from kings down to the common people. This was partly due to the fact that the journey overland had been greatly facilitated by the

PREVIOUS: The breathtaking interior of the Church of Sainte-Chapelle in Paris, built in the 1240s especially to house the Crown of Thorns and other relics of Christ brought back from the Crusades. The chapel itself has been likened to a giant reliquary.

Christianization of Hungary during the reign of King Stephen (997–1038). He enforced clerical discipline and built monasteries, churches and pilgrim hostels, causing Glaber to remark that the Hungarians had turned from cruel predators into people who 'give freely of their own for the sake of Christ' (a judgment that was for a time undermined by Stephen's pagan successors). In 1026 a band of some 700 pilgrims sponsored by the Duke of Normandy made their way to the Holy Land; and in 1064 some 12,000 souls travelled there from Germany. Led by the Bishop of Bamberg, the pilgrims reached Palestine via Constantinople, surviving a fierce attack by local Bedouins at the town of Capernaum. With hindsight, this pilgrim journey seems almost like a rehearsal for the Crusades, thirty-five years later.

Although they continued in an increasingly attenuated form until the end of the Middle Ages and even beyond, the Crusades were at their most intense for their first 100 years. They were inextricably linked with pilgrimage: the Crusaders' avowed aim was to prise Christianity's shrines from the grasp of the Muslims and to safeguard the journeys of pilgrims; and they themselves were considered to be pilgrims, albeit of a martial kind. Like their non-bellicose counterparts, Crusaders took a solemn vow to undertake their journeys, the breaking of which could result in excommunication; they also received a badge in the form of a cross from the Church authorities, marking them as soldiers of Christ. In return for their service, they were promised indulgences, the customary reward of pilgrimage (see pages 66–7). There was also, of course, the prospect of land and booty; and for many of Europe's more restless high-born youths the combination of spiritual and temporal incentives proved irresistible.

The initial spur for the Crusades occurred when the Seljuk Turks took control of Palestine towards the end of the eleventh century, and with their aggressive policies made pilgrimage there almost impossible. After Pope Urban II's great rallying call in 1095, the First Crusade was set in motion, ending with the Christians' capture of Jerusalem in 1099. For the next 200 years there was a permanent, although diminishing, Christian presence in Palestine. Crusader states such as the earldoms of Edessa and Tripoli, and the kingdom of Jerusalem, were carved out, and pilgrim traffic resumed. The Crusaders set about rebuilding Jerusalem, founding churches, monasteries and convents; and in the 1140s they enlarged the Church of the Holy Sepulchre, uniting the previously separate sites of Jesus' death and resurrection under one roof. It was also about this time that the two great Christian military orders of the Knights Hospitaller and Knights Templar developed, at first to give protection and hospitality to pilgrims (the Hospitallers built an enormous hospice in Jerusalem that could hold some 2,000 pilgrims), then as fully-fledged professional armies.

The Second Crusade, launched in 1147 to recapture Edessa after its loss to the Muslims three years earlier, ended in failure. The Third Crusade (1189–92), prompted by the loss of Jerusalem, was only a partial success, with Richard I, the Lion-Heart, unable to retake Jerusalem but managing to force concessions from his adversary Saladin. The Fourth Crusade (1202–04), the last of the major expeditions, aimed to invade Egypt – but at the prompting of Venice the army of Catholic Latin warriors was diverted to fight against the Orthodox Christians of Byzantine Constantinople (Venice's great trading rival). In a three-day orgy of violence the Crusaders murdered, raped and looted their way through the city, leaving a trail of bitterness preserved in Greek consciousness to this day (in 2001 Pope John Paul II apologized to the Greek Orthodox Church for this 800-year-old outrage).

One outcome of the Crusaders' looting was the redistribution of Constantinople's thousands of relics to the West, where they helped to revitalize old shrines and create new ones. One Latin monk is said to have stolen from the Church of the Pantocrator a splinter of the True Cross, the arm of St James, a tooth of St Lawrence, a foot of St Cosmas and more than thirty other remains of saints. The precious Crown of Thorns ended up in Paris, where Louis IX built for it the beautiful Sainte-Chapelle. Another fragment of the True Cross reached the small Cluniac priory of Bromholm in Norfolk, England, in 1223 and transformed it into an important pilgrimage centre. Almost immediately the relic was said to be effecting miracles – 'the blind saw, the lame walked, the lepers were cleansed' – and in time Bromholm received visits and patronage from nobles and kings, including Henry III, Edward II and Henry V. Such was the power of this sacred splinter that it continued to draw pilgrims to the priory until its closure at the Reformation.

A fifteenth-century manuscript illumination showing the Crusaders – in the guise of later medieval soldiers – looting Jerusalem after capturing it in 1099.

PILGRIMAGE AND THE AFTERLIFE

In the Middle Ages pilgrimage was inextricably bound up with other religious concerns of the time, particularly indulgences, purgatory, holy relics and the cult of saints, all of which connected the pilgrim to the realm of the afterlife and the deceased. Two common motives for making pilgrimages were to ask help from the saints in heaven through contact with their holy relics on earth and to gain an indulgence – the remission of a certain amount of temporal punishment due to sin, either in this life or in purgatory after death. The fate of the individual in the afterlife and the nature of heaven, hell and especially purgatory was of paramount concern to medieval Christians. Indeed, historian Eamon Duffy has remarked that 'there is a case for saying the defining doctrine of late medieval Catholicism was purgatory'. In short, people believed that when they died they went to one of three 'places': hell if they were unrepentant sinners, heaven if they were truly righteous and purgatory if they fell between the saintly and the damned – which meant nearly everyone. The rewards of saints and of sinners were graphically broadcast through sermons, church frescoes and carvings, manuscript illuminations and written accounts that depicted the tortures and blessings of the afterlife. Some writings were literary creations, such as Dante's *Divine Comedy*, others were penned or inspired by individuals who claimed to have had visions of the world to come.

Bede tells the story of a Northumbrian man named Drycthelm, who became a monk at Melrose in Scotland after receiving a vision of the afterlife. Drycthelm said that an angelic guide had taken him to a terrifying valley where people's souls were tossed from one side, where fires raged, to the other, where snow and hail swirled around. He was then led away to a dark place where, amid a terrible stench and the sound of demonic laughter and cries of agony, black flames bearing the souls of men 'like sparks' streamed up and down from a pit. To his relief, Drycthelm was then taken by his guide to a fragrant meadow where people dressed in white robes were sitting happily. From there they passed to the threshold of another place where the sweet

This twelfth-century tympanum of the Last Judgment, above the entrance to the Cathedral of Saint-Lazare at Autun in France, presents a powerful illustration of the potential rewards and punishments of the afterlife.

singing and the lovely scent and light were too wonderful to describe. The guide then told Drycthelm that the valley was where souls who were penitent only at the hour of their death had to stay before being admitted to heaven; that the pit was the mouth of hell; the meadow was for souls who had been good when alive but did not deserve immediate entry into heaven; and the place of light was heaven itself.

Although purgatory – Drycthelm's valley – did not claim the dead for eternity, as hell was thought to do, it was still a terrifying prospect. St Thomas Aquinas remarked that no pain on earth came near the torment of its fire. But how and when did the idea of purgatory arise? There is some evidence for such a place in classical literature and the Old Testament. In Virgil's *Aeneid* the hero Aeneas enters the underworld where the ghost of his father Anchises tells him about the mysteries of the dead and how souls are punished for old sins – some have their wickedness washed away, others have it burnt out of them – before being allowed to enter Elysium. In the Old

Testament, purgatory is suggested in The Second Book of Maccabbees 12:39–45 when Judas and his troops pray for their dead comrades so that their sin (of wearing magic amulets) might be 'entirely blotted out'. Judas also sends a collection of money to Jerusalem to be offered for their sin – an action, as Christian commentators have argued, that presupposes that the dead could benefit from it.

Christians also found justifications for purgatory in Church tradition and in the New Testament, such as Jesus' warning in Matthew 12:32 that he who speaks against the Holy Spirit will not be forgiven in this world or in the world to come. And St Paul in his First Letter to the Corinthians 3:11–15 seems to imply a post-mortem state where souls will be purified by fire. There was also the age-old custom of praying for the dead, evident, for example, in inscriptions on tombs in the Roman catacombs: why pray for the departed, it was argued, unless they could be helped by prayer? St Augustine of Hippo summed it up by stating that prayer could help the dead who were not so wicked while alive that they forfeited compassion, nor so good that they did not need it at all. This was the same view as that of Drycthelm's angelic guide, who said that 'many are helped by the prayers, alms and fasting of the living, and especially by the offerings of masses, and are therefore set free before the Day of Judgment'.

Behind these beliefs was the idea of unfulfilled penance (the word comes from poena, Latin for 'punishment'). Although the Church had the power to absolve repentant sinners who confessed their wrongdoings of guilt, the miscreants were still obliged to do a penance, such as undertake a fast or a pilgrimage. During the reign of King Canute (1016–35) it was decreed that anyone who killed a priest was to be outlawed unless he atoned for the act 'by pilgrimage and also towards the kindred' of the deceased. But what happened if people died before doing their penitential punishment? The Church's answer was that they would suffer it in purgatory, where they would be purged, or spiritually purified, before being admitted to the ranks of the blessed. The dead could shorten their time in purgatory, however, if the living prayed or said masses for them. Margery Kempe remarked that the soul of her husband would remain in purgatory for thirty years 'unless he had better friends on

A detail from *The Last Judgment* (c. 1431) by Fra Angelico showing the torment of the damned unrepentant sinners suffering eternal penance for their sins on earth.

earth'. St Bridget of Sweden was mystically informed that many souls in purgatory had been freed by her pious acts in the Church of the Holy Sepulchre. And many a will was drawn up to ensure that money would be available for pilgrimages or other acts of piety to be performed on behalf of the deceased. Those who could afford it also often founded chantry chapels so that prayers could be said for their souls.

PENANCE AND INDULGENCES

The idea of indulgences was also connected with the system of penance. Over a period of time the Church recognized that some penances, particularly the longer ones, could be disruptive to the rhythms and tasks of everyday life, such as ploughing or harvesting, and allowed them to be commuted. So the short, sharp shock of a flogging could be substituted for a long pilgrimage, or singing psalms while bending the knees could take the place of a month-long fast on bread and water. In civil courts it was not uncommon for the convicted to pay a fine instead of the pilgrimage to which they had been sentenced. Books known as *Penitentials* set out precisely the relative values of penances. That of Egbert, the eighth-century archbishop of York, for example, stated that reciting fifty psalms kneeling down was the equivalent of fasting on bread and water for a day, and that a year-long fast could be reduced by the payment of twenty-five shillings.

From about the late eleventh century onwards, indulgences of specific value were assigned to certain pious acts, relics, shrines and pilgrimages. It was said that two pilgrimages to St David's Cathedral in Wales were worth the virtue of one to Rome. In the late fourteenth century to travel to Rome to pray before the relic known as the Veronica (see pages 87) was worth 12,000 years remission of purgatorial punishment (but only 3,000 if you were a Roman citizen). Noticeboards outside churches and shrines advertized their indulgences, and handbooks known as *libri indulgentiarum* were produced to list the indulgences attached to each shrine or relic. When Gerald of Wales made a pilgrimage to Rome in about 1204, he was able to calculate that during his stay he had earned indulgences worth ninety-two years. Naturally, proprietors of shrines vied with each other to pay their bishops or the pope for the privilege of dispensing indulgences, hoping to recoup their investment by the offerings of increased numbers of pilgrims. There were also plenary indulgences, which offered a complete remission of penance. The first of these was given by Pope Urban II at the Council of

Clermont in 1095 to those joining the First Crusade. In 1300, to celebrate the Jubilee Year (see pages 96–7), Pope Boniface VIII granted a plenary indulgence to all pilgrims who came to Rome, a practice repeated in subsequent Jubilee Years.

Eventually, it became increasingly common for individuals to be able to buy indulgences without having to go to a shrine or see a relic. For those who were too sick or old – or too preoccupied – to go on a pilgrimage or crusade, or who could not find a substitute person to go for them, indulgences were a boon. Nevertheless, although much of the money raised often went to good causes, such as the building of a hospice or bridge, the practice was open to abuse by the rich and idle, who found it easier to buy post-mortem remissions of punishment than earn them by physical hardship, and by those who were only too keen to make money out of selling indulgences, including cash-strapped popes such as Boniface IX (1389–1404). Official indulgence sellers known as 'pardoners' became a familiar sight in towns and villages, where they used emotive rhetoric, impressive-looking documents and collections of relics to persuade people to reduce their stint of purgatorial punishment – at a fee. The Church recognized these faults: the Lateran Council of 1215, for example, declared that bishops could only give indulgences worth a maximum of one year and only to those who had attended the consecration of a church; and in 1418 the Council of Constance also tried to restrict them. Nevertheless, the abuses continued up to the Reformation.

THE CULT OF RELICS

According to his medieval biographer, Hugh, a twelfth-century bishop of Lincoln, was visiting the monastery of Fécamp in Normandy when he asked to see the monks' prize relic – the arm of Mary Magdalene. With the monks in attendance Hugh proceeded to take the arm, cut away its covering and try to break off a piece of the bone, but in vain. Nothing daunted he snatched up the arm and bit off a finger with his teeth – much to the horror of the monks, who compared him to a dog with a bone. It was not that Hugh – who managed to mollify his hosts – was a brutish lout. Rather, he was a man famous for his piety, love for humanity and kindness to lepers, who was canonized twenty years after his death. What the incident shows is the importance relics assumed in medieval life.

Relics were the tangible remains of a saint whose intercessions with the Almighty offered the hope of miraculous cures and good fortune. In an age when people took for granted the power of the supernatural and believed that common and uncommon occurrences, from sprained ankles to lightning bolts and plagues, were governed by God, relics were generally regarded as manifestations of the spiritual. They were objects of awe, and were often used instead of the Bible for the taking of oaths. As such, relics were the heart of a shrine and its crown jewels. They had the power to lure pilgrims across seas and over mountains and, when they arrived, to persuade them to part with their money. The arrival of a relic could raise a shrine from obscurity to fame and prosperity, as had happened to the priory of Bromholm in Norfolk. So the desire for relics was constant, and competition to obtain them could be intense to the point of illegality. It was not uncommon for the guardians of one shrine to steal them from another, and stories of wonder-working relics were used as propaganda by rival sanctuaries.

The involvement of relics in the life of the Church goes back to the early days of Christianity. By the early Middle Ages they had become standard items in worship. Bede tells how Pope Gregory I sent Augustine of Canterbury everything he would need for church services in England, including vestments, books, vessels, ornaments, altar cloths and 'relics of the holy Apostles and martyrs'. In 787, about fifty years after Bede's death, the Second Council of Nicaea increased the need for relics by enjoining that henceforth no church could be consecrated without them. The constantly increasing demand was fed during the period of the Crusades by the great number of relics from Jerusalem, Antioch and other places in the Holy Land that made their way back to Europe.

Over time some relics gained more fame and prestige than others, attracting pilgrims from far and wide. These included the tunic of the Virgin Mary at Chartres; the skulls of the three Magi at Cologne; the remains of St James at Compostela; and of course the remains of St Peter and St Paul at Rome. There were tens of thousands of lesser known relics scattered in churches and shrines throughout Europe: nails and splinters from the True Cross (enough to build a ship, as the Renaissance scholar and satirist Erasmus remarked); bones, teeth, hair and nail clippings of countless saints; phials containing the blood or even the breath of Jesus, or the milk of the Virgin Mary; bits of cloth from Mary's tunic, and so on. There were said to be some 700 known spikes from the Crown of Thorns. The one kept at Angers was actually a thorn that had merely touched the 'real' Crown, suggesting a belief in the transference of spiritual power that may account for other multiplications of relics, such as the holy nails of the Cross, of which there were at least thirty in existence.

These sacred objects were usually kept in resplendent reliquaries, ranging from large gold-plated chests encrusted with jewels, such as at St Thomas Becket's shrine at Canterbury, to gilt arm-shaped cases enclosing the arm bones of saints or small pendants containing strands of holy hair. Reliquaries were designed to inspire awe and were displayed or carried in procession on special occasions such as feast days or at times of plague or national crisis. Visual impact, in an age of widespread illiteracy, played an important part in religion: what pilgrims expected to see was something opulent and lustrous that would convey in physical terms the essence of the shrine's and saint's spirituality. They were not as concerned, as most modern pilgrims would tend to be, with the authenticity of the relics or whether they had been stolen from another shrine. What mattered was their relationship with the relic and how it connected them to the departed saint and through him or her to Christ in heaven.

The nature of this relationship, and whether, for example, it was based on idolatry, was a point of issue for theologians. St Thomas Aquinas, following St Jerome and St Augustine, wrote that it was normal to honour objects connected with people who had themselves been held in honour, and so it was natural to venerate the bodies of saints: 'God fittingly does honour to such relics by performing miracles in their presence.' Relics, therefore, were not simply objects of magic that worked their power indifferently, but receptacles of the holy presence 'through which,' as the Council of

ABOVE The twelfth-century reliquary of St Stephen made of gilded copper with enamel work, housed in his shrine in Limoges Cathedral, France.

Trent (1545–63) later pronounced, 'many benefits are bestowed on mankind'. Inevitably, however, the incessant demand for relics by religious institutions and by wealthy individuals helped to create and sustain a trade in which the distinctions between 'false' and 'true' relics became blurred. The Church acknowledged the problem: as far back as the fourth century St Augustine had inveighed against itinerants dressed as monks who were living off the sale of false relics. But it was not always easy for the Church authorities to determine between the false and the genuine. One method was to see whether or not the relic burned (true relics were believed to resist fire): a tenth-century bishop of Trier tested the alleged body of St Celsus during Mass by casting part of the saint's finger into a censer of burning coals, which apparently did it no harm.

In the thirteenth century a General Church Council at Lyons formally pronounced that recently found relics should not be venerated unless approved by the pope. Such a decree recognized a problem even if it could not solve it. In the next century Chaucer satirized the trade in false relics through his portrait of a pardoner whose relic collection included a pillow case which he claimed to be the veil of the Virgin Mary and various 'pigges bones'. The Italian poet Boccaccio also portrayed a pardoner, who had a parrot's feather that he pretended had come from the Angel Gabriel. Although these examples were intended to amuse, they reflect the fact that spurious relics were commonplace. Just how commonplace may be inferred from the inventory of relics made in 1523 at the church of Wittenberg, the epicentre of the Reformation: it showed that here, Frederick, Elector of Saxony, had accumulated some 17,000 objects of veneration. The Reformers had no time for relics, purgatory or the cult of the saints (see pages 130–35). For them the Word of God was paramount and any practice not supported by the scriptures was at the very least suspect. Their attitude may be summed up by Erasmus, who wrote: 'You make much of a piece of his body visible through a glass covering and you do not marvel at the whole mind of Paul shining through his writings?'

A ninth-century reliquary of St Foy, in gold and precious stones, at Sainte-Foy Abbey in Conques, France. The statuette encloses the relics of the saint.

ON THE ROAD

Before embarking on a long-distance pilgrimage, a medieval pilgrim had to make certain preparations. In a society characterized by a hierarchical structure and a web of relationships based on services owed or owing, it was necessary first of all to obtain permission to leave home from the local bishop, abbot, parish priest, feudal lord or other authority. The German monk Felix Fabri, (see pages 117–121), for example, had to obtain permission from Pope Sixtus IV as well as from senior members of his Dominican order; and when Margery Kempe was on pilgrimage in York she was interrogated by Church officials as to whether she had written permission from her husband to be there. In England in 1388, Richard II's government decreed on pain of arrest that pilgrims should have special permits as well as passports if they wished to travel abroad. Port officials who turned a blind eye to unlicensed pilgrims were liable to severe punishment. Official authorization to travel was not only to the benefit of the governing classes keeping tabs on their inferiors. In an age when roads were frequented by an assortment of itinerant travellers, from wealthy merchants to beggars and vagabonds, it was to the pilgrim's great advantage if he had documentary proof of his purpose. Documents showed that pilgrims were not spies or outlaws or labourers illegally wandering off to seek employment with another landowner. In most countries, at least in principle, special protection was given to pilgrims as well as other legal privileges, such as exemption from certain tolls along the way.

Since pilgrimages to faraway shrines would probably involve dangers of one sort or another, the prudent pilgrim would settle his affairs before leaving home. Debts were paid, a will was drawn up and provision made for dependants. Margery Kempe, for example, asked her parish priest to announce in church that she was going on pilgrimage and that her creditors should come and see her before her departure. The would-be traveller would also get hold of the pilgrim's traditional clothes and accessories. These comprised a wide-brimmed hat, which gave good protection from

The Italian Pellegrini family coat of arms, from a fresco in St Anastasia, Verona.
It depicts a well-equipped pilgrim with a heavy coat, strong boots, a long staff
and a broad-brimmed hat bearing the pilgrim's scallop-shell badge.

sun and rain; a scrip, which was a small leather satchel in which documents, money, food and knick-knacks were kept; a stout staff, which served as an alpenstock when climbing mountains, as a pole for vaulting across streams and as a weapon against brigands or fierce dogs; and a long thick cloak that could double as a blanket. Strong boots or shoes were indispensable, as was a water bottle or leather beaker.

These pilgrim items were not of purely practical value. Before a pilgrim's departure, the staff and scrip were blessed by a priest in a church ceremony, so that they would give spiritual protection. According to the instructions of the *Sarum Missal* of 1554, the pilgrim first confessed his or her sins, then lay on the floor before the altar as the priest and choir sang suitable psalms such as the twenty-fourth, which has the lines: 'Who shall ascend into the hill of the Lord? Who shall stand in his holy place? He that hath clean hands, and a pure heart; who hath not lifted up his soul unto vanity, nor sworn deceitfully.' The priest then blessed the scrip and the staff, invoking the protection of Christ. He sprinkled holy water on the scrip and, uttering more prayers, placed it round the pilgrim's neck. He anointed the staff too, and handed it over with the words: 'Take this staff as a support during your journey and the toils of your pilgrimage, that you may be victorious against the bands of the enemy and safely arrive at the shrine of the saints to which you wish to go and, your journey accomplished, may return to us in good health.' Pilgrims bound for Jerusalem would usually have cloth crosses blessed and anointed with water and then sewn on to their hats and cloaks before the congregation. Some of the pilgrim items also acquired symbolic value, a tendency perhaps best known from Sir Walter Raleigh's poem 'The Passionate Man's Pilgrimage': 'Give me my scallop-shell of quiet,/My staff of faith to walk upon,/My scrip of joy, immortal diet,/My bottle of salvation,/My gown of glory, hope's true gage;/And thus I'll take my pilgrimage.'

Because pilgrims could be away for months – a typical journey from London to Rome and back could take from three to five months depending on conditions – they had to ensure they had enough money for food and lodging, for making offerings at shrines and for buying souvenirs. For the poor this meant saving up for years on end, unless they were lucky enough to find a wealthy patron. Some landed pilgrims made over some or all of their property to a monastery or other landowner in exchange for cash. Another source of funding might be a trade or religious guild. In Lincoln, members of the religious Guild of the Resurrection were obliged to give a halfpenny to anyone wanting to make a pilgrimage to Rome, Compostela or Jerusalem; and members of the tailors' guild each gave a penny to those bound for the Holy Land. These offerings were not entirely altruistic: by the act of giving, those unable to make the pilgrimage could identify themselves with it and share the virtue accrued by the pilgrim in the fulfilment of the journey.

The actual sendoff could be small and low-key or involve a cheering crowd of family, friends and fellow guild members, who accompanied the pilgrim to the city gate or other landmark. Since it was accepted that a pilgrim might not survive a long-distance journey, emotional farewells must have been common. Felix Fabri gives a good insight into the thoughts and feelings of one who was about to embark on such pilgrimage. When he announced his intention to go to the Holy Land, during a sermon held in Ulm in April 1480, the congregation's singing was punctuated by loud sobs as people realized the implications of his plan. On 15 April Felix finally set off for Venice (from where he would proceed by galley to Jerusalem), but not before he had 'rushed into the arms' of his 'most kind and beloved spiritual father'. The two men embraced each other, their cheeks wet with tears. Then, as he set off, Felix felt what many other pilgrims must have felt before and after him – a deep sense of futility and a sudden nostalgia for home and familiar things. The ardour with which he yearned to see the Holy Land not only cooled but 'died' within him, and the pilgrimage seemed 'useless' and 'empty', the memory of Ulm so much sweeter than the prospect of Jerusalem.

HAZARDS OF THE WAY

Travelling on land, medieval pilgrims would normally proceed on foot, or by horse, donkey or mule, or in a wagon. They would cover approximately fifteen to twenty-five miles a day if they were walking; or from twenty to thirty miles riding at a 'canter', a word supposedly derived from 'Canterbury trot' and used to describe the gentle pace at which pilgrims travelled (in the case of Chaucer's pilgrims slow enough for them to be able to chat and listen to stories). Each day pilgrims aimed to arrive at an inn, monastery or hospice before night fell, otherwise the sheer intensity of darkness – almost unimaginable now in most parts of the developed world – coupled with a lack of good road signs and maps might prove their undoing. There was also danger from wolves and other wild animals. It is said that when Sturmi, an eighth-century abbot of Fulda in Germany, was travelling through the wild terrain around his monastery he had to chop down trees at the end of each day and make a stockade to protect his horse.

In medieval Europe roads were often no more than rubble tracks. Gone were the days of ancient Rome when paved roads crisscrossed the empire in straight military lines. There was no consistent central policy for maintaining roads. In fourteenth-century England, they were the responsibility of local landlords and their condition was subject to the landlord's wealth and whim. Yet the construction of roads and bridges came to be viewed as a holy and virtuous duty, an act of charity comparable to giving money to the poor. It was at least partly in this spirit that the abbey of Cluny financed improvements and repairs to the road to Santiago de Compostela, facilitating access for pilgrims. Nevertheless, the Crown sometimes had to intervene if the local authorities failed to fulfil their responsibilities. Charles VI of France was forced to act when the roads around Paris had deteriorated into an obstacle course of boulders and deep ruts, with trees growing in the middle of the road, and hedges and brambles encroaching from the sides. The king ordered the Provost of Paris to carry out the necessary clearances and repairs, authorizing him to press-gang local labour if required.

Apart from the state of the roads, pilgrims and other travellers had to contend with robbers and brigands, who knew the pilgrim routes well and could easily pick off a lone pilgrim then melt back quickly into the surrounding woods or undergrowth. The Pilgrim's Way, from Winchester to Canterbury, passed by the notorious Alice Holt Woods, between Alton and Farnham, where robbers preyed on travellers. On the days that St Giles' Fair was held in Winchester mounted guards were sent by the fair's authorities to protect incoming merchants. Another measure to foil ambushes and muggings was taken in 1285 by Edward I, who ordered roadsides to be cleared by no less than 200 feet to deprive malefactors of potential hiding places. Pilgrims also had

In *The Path of Life*, part of a triptych painted in the 1480s, Hieronymus Bosch gives an allegorical meaning to some of the real trials that medieval pilgrims faced. Bosch's traveller through life faces sin, death and persecution on all sides.

to contend with ongoing wars or civil strife. In the Holy Land, even after the Crusaders' conquests, Bedouin tribesmen were known to swoop down on unsuspecting pilgrim bands. Some pilgrims of high rank prudently adopted humbler dress, the better to travel unnoticed. Certainly, a change of identity seems to have saved the skin of an English monk named Samson in 1161. He was travelling in Italy en route to Rome when he found himself caught up in fighting between Pope Alexander III and Emperor Frederick I, whose men were mutilating those they found travelling to the pope. Samson managed to ward off attackers by pretending to be a Scot, brandishing his stick at them 'in the manner of a weapon called a gaveloc' and growling threats 'in the Scottish manner'.

If roads could sometimes be as much a hindrance as a medium of progress another potential impediment to pilgrims was rivers. In the absence of a bridge, and if the river was not too wide or deep, travellers could wade across, perhaps aided by a rope strung from bank to bank. If the river was too deep the only other way of crossing it was by ferry, which could also be a life-endangering experience. The twelfth-century *Pilgrim's Guide* to Compostela tells of the boatmen of two rivers south of Gascony in France who extracted high charges for their services by force and whose boats were so small – carved from single tree trunks – that passengers were terrified the vessels would capsize (the *Guide* goes so far as to accuse the boatmen of deliberate overcrowding in order to drown passengers and steal their belongings). Even if ferrymen were not actively malign they might be prone to misjudgment or careless greed. In the twelfth century, a number of fatal accidents connected with the ferry service across the River Arno in Italy prompted the saintly Allucius of Pescia to petition the local bishop to build a bridge. And a German woman crossing the Rhône on her way back from Compostela found herself on a large boat packed with about 400 people and their horses and donkeys. As soon as the vessel hit a patch of choppy water the weight proved too much: it shipped water and sank. The woman was the only survivor.

Conditions of travel could be just as precarious in the mountains, especially the Alps, where a constant flow of pilgrims negotiated the vertiginous icy passes on their way to or from Rome. Experienced local guides, properly equipped with studded boots, were indispensable. Nonetheless, travellers often had to swap dignity for necessity and scrabble on all fours over the slippery frozen tracks. Home-made sledges made out of oxhides or branches tied together were used. Wagons had to be let down gently by rope, counterbalanced by teams of men or oxen. Avalanches were a constant hazard: in 1128 two Belgian abbots witnessed a fall of snow on the alpine village of Saint-Rémy in which houses were swallowed up and inhabitants and travellers buried alive.

Travel overland had its discomforts and dangers; passage by ship was often worse. Pilgrim vessels regularly departed from Venice to Palestine and from English ports such as Bristol, Dartmouth and Southampton to northern Spain and Compostela. Life on board ship for landlubbers was usually disconcerting and often distressing. For first-time voyagers the whining creak of timbers, the sudden crashing of waves and the stink from the bilges were a novel form of torture. Food was often maggot-ridden and drinking water discoloured and malodorous. A fifteenth-century English poem called 'The Pilgrims' Sea Voyage' describes how gruesome the journey to Compostela could be: the seasick pilgrims groan and vomit or shout for Malmsey wine to settle their stomachs; some peck at a little salted toast, others try in vain to read. The poem ends with the pilgrim narrator thinking fondly of dry land and cursing the smell from the bilge pump: 'I had as lefe be in the wood/Without mete and drynk;/For when that we shall go to bedde,/The pumpe was nygh oure beddes hede,/A man were as good to be dede/As smell thereof the stynk!'

Journeys to Palestine were no better, as Felix Fabri vividly describes (see page 121). As well as the heat, smell, cramped conditions and sudden Mediterranean storms, there was also the routine threat of Saracen pirates. A German chronicle records that in 1453 a ship returning from Palestine with about 300 pilgrims was set upon by Saracens, who killed the men and enslaved the women.

But journeys by sea could be improved a good deal – if you knew how. The seasoned fifteenth-century English pilgrim William Wey recorded some sensible tips. He recommended that pilgrims to Jerusalem should negotiate with the ship's captain for a place on the top deck, the lowest one being 'ryght smolderyng hote and stynkynge'. Before the start of the voyage the pilgrim should buy certain items such as sheets, pillows, a mattress and a quilt. A good chest with a lock was essential, and a little cauldron, a frying pan, plates, wooden saucers, cups and a bread grater would not come amiss. It was sensible to take a cage with half a dozen hens, as well as a range

of medical remedies such as 'laxatives' and 'restoratives', and various spices such as ginger, pepper, saffron and cloves to make the food more palatable and to ease digestion. With purchases such as these, wealthier late medieval pilgrims could make conditions on board quite tolerable.

PLACES TO STAY EN ROUTE

As a day of travelling drew to an end, pilgrims would hope to find themselves near appropriate accommodation. Their long thick cloaks gave them the option of bedding down under a tree, but for protection from the elements and safety – though not always comfort – a monastery guesthouse, hospice or inn were the desirable destinations. Monasteries were obliged in theory to give free board and lodging for up to three days to pilgrims and other wayfarers. According to the Rule of St Benedict, guests at monasteries were to be received as if they were Christ himself, and their feet washed by the abbot and his brethren. However, the hierarchical nature of medieval society meant that guests received the degree of hospitality appropriate to their station, as shown by the monastery of St Gall in Switzerland, which had separate accommodation for the poor, visiting monks and VIPs, who were assigned their own well-heated house with a kitchen, wine cellar and bakery.

Along well-trodden pilgrim routes and other major thoroughfares basic accommodation for pilgrims was provided by hostels known as *hospitia*, or hospices, many of them founded by philanthropic nobles or the Knights Hospitaller. The three most famous hospices, according to the *Pilgrim's Guide* to Compostela, were in Jerusalem, at the Great St Bernard Pass in the Alps and at the Somport Pass in the Pyrenees. Several nations, including the Spanish, Swedish and English, established their own hospices in Rome for the use of poor pilgrims from their respective countries. The English, in fact, had two hospices, one dedicated to St Thomas of Canterbury, the other to St Edmund, which by 1449 had grown to incorporate nine houses along with gardens and vineyards.

The Peasant Wedding (*c.* 1568) by Pieter Bruegel the Elder shows the sort of hostelry a late medieval pilgrim might hope to reach at the end of a day's travelling. Food, drink and entertainment refreshed the spirit as well as the body.

For pilgrims who had a bit of money, inns and taverns could prove a more congenial alternative. Inns ranged from small, dingy hovels to relatively grand establishments that might offer not only board, lodging and stabling but also medicines and a laundry service. It was common practice for guests to share not only rooms but also beds. Each bed usually slept a minimum of two, though three to five people sharing was not uncommon – a fourteenth-century French traveller remarked that German inns customarily assigned three to a bed. In England, an inn in the town of Ware named 'The Saracen's Head' had the so-called Great Bed, which measured eleven feet long by ten feet wide and was said to hold twenty people – though perhaps it was more of a soft 'landing area' for drunks to collapse on. Bedding could range from straw-stuffed mattresses to a heap of dried bracken; fleas, bed bugs, rats and mice were an occupational hazard.

A typical inn consisted of a communal area with tables and a fireplace, a kitchen, the private quarters of the landlord and his family, and a room or rooms for guests. Food at humble establishments included staples such as soup, bread, cheese, eggs and poultry, while large inns in cities might provide more variety and spices to pep up the fare. They might also supply in-house entertainment in the form of local musicians or buskers, who passed a hat round after the performance. Felix Fabri describes an evening in an inn in Trent in northern Italy, en route to Venice in 1483, when he and his entourage were entertained by a local craftsman and his wife, who sang, played the flute and clowned around, much to the hilarity of the diners. In England inns were supplemented by the alehouse or 'ale-stake', recognizable by the long pole projecting from above the door, its tip garlanded with brushwood. Frequently found at crossroads as well as by the wayside, ale-stakes tended to be little more than humble shacks. Some offered ale alone, while others also provided basic victuals, as Chaucer's pardoner bears witness: 'But first, he said, here at this ale-stake/I will both drink and bite upon a cake.'

In large cities some inns were run by expatriates, who especially welcomed the custom of their fellow countrymen. In Venice the gathering place for Germans was the St George, where even the servants were German or at least German-speaking. When Felix Fabri visited it in 1483 he noted that the landlord's big black dog welcomed German visitors by jumping up and wagging his tail. Only Germans, however, and respectable ones at that, were shown such warmth. Beggars and foreigners – including the native Italians – provoked growls and barking. Innkeepers themselves were frequently the objects of complaint – not all of them were like genial Harry Bailey, the host of the Tabard Inn in the *Canterbury Tales*. Many gained a dubious reputation for charging too much for their services, especially when occasions such as Jubilee Years increased the number of pilgrims. In 1235 measures passed by the Senate in Rome attempted to halt the innkeepers' practice of physically forcing pilgrims inside their inns or snatching them from rival taverns; and in England during the reign of Edward III (1327–77) a statute was passed to prevent innkeepers selling their food at extortionate prices.

Of course, being able to speak a few words of the local language was invaluable for negotiating with hostellers, if not their dogs. Although educated pilgrims would normally speak Latin to their peers, they and their uneducated brethren would have to learn a little of the vernacular if they wanted to communicate with the locals. This could be extremely difficult in some areas. The *Pilgrim's Guide* to Compostela splenetically describes the Basque language as 'barbarous', citing as evidence examples of individual words: 'bread' is *orgui*, 'water' *uric* and 'corn' *gari*. One time-honoured alternative to speech was sign language; another was to resort to a phrase book, a genre that became increasingly popular towards the end of the Middle Ages. *Conversations in Old High-German*, for instance, was intended for travellers from Romance countries visiting Germany and included useful phrases such as 'I would like drink', 'Have you any fodder for my horse?' and 'My shoe needs mending'. There were also phrases such as 'The Latin people are stupid, but the Bavarians are wise', which show, as historian Norbert Ohler has noted, 'that the Romance speaking author knew how to gain the sympathy of the "natives"'. William Wey obligingly recorded Greek phrases that could be used on the voyage to Jerusalem in places like the islands of Crete, Rhodes and Cyprus. Some of these resemble in sound the Greek spoken today, such as: 'Good morning', *Calomare* 'How much?', *Posso?*; and 'Woman, have you got any good wine?', *Geneca esse calocrasse?* Wey also noted some Arabic phrases, as did the anonymous author of the fifteenth-century English *Informacyon for Pylgrymes*. By this period there were also French–Arabic phrase books for Francophone travellers.

Arriving and Departing

When pilgrims finally reached the end of their journey and arrived at the shrine that had for days, weeks or months been the focus of their hopes, it was clearly a moment of intense emotion. Just how intense can be glimpsed from Felix Fabri's description of the wailing, sobbing and convulsive fits of his fellow pilgrims at the threshold of the Church of the Holy Sepulchre in Jerusalem in 1483. For many pilgrims cathedral shrines would have been the largest and most magnificent buildings they had ever seen. The profusion of soaring columns, paintings and carvings of biblical scenes, stained-glass windows, chapels, altars and golden bejewelled shrines bathed in the flickering light of candles must have been an unprecedented sensory experience.

During the pilgrim season and especially on saints' feast days, shrines could be crowded, noisy and chaotic. An anonymous fourteenth-century English visitor to St Peter's in Rome said that a pilgrim might have to search all day for a lost companion, so vast was the church and so great the number of visitors running hither and thither, collecting indulgences at various shrines and altars. The sick pressed their way towards the shrine on crutches; the paralysed on hand-trestles, or carried on stretchers and in wheel barrows; the blind were led by their companions. It was believed that the nearer an invalid got to the relics, the greater the chance of a cure – so some tried to sleep on the shrine or tomb itself. All-night vigils in the shrine could be boisterous affairs. Apart from the cries of the infirm and the shouts of those who thought themselves possessed by demons there might also be loud uninhibited praying and singing. The *Pilgrim's Guide* to Compostela describes such a scene in the cathedral there as pilgrims from France, Germany, Italy and other countries gathered together in groups, holding so many candles aloft that the church seemed to be bathed in daylight. In the general hubbub people wept for their sins or read psalms aloud, some gossiped or ate picnics, while others sang in their native languages, accompanied by lyres, timbrels, flutes, harps and other instruments.

Sometimes the crowds could get out of hand. In the twelfth century, Abbot Suger

A painting of pilgrims gathering close to the shrine of St Wolfgang in Regensburg, Austria. Wax votive offerings have been left by earlier visitors and the number of abandoned crutches testify to the number of pilgrims healed at the shrine.

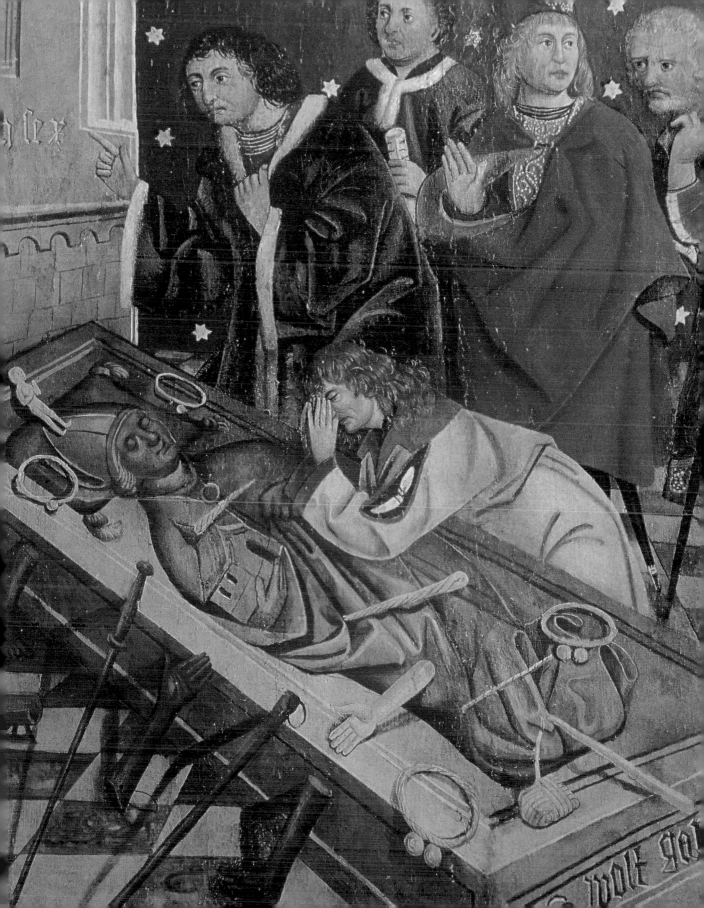

of the monastery of St Denis, near Paris, described how on feast days pilgrims would pack themselves into the monastery's church to view the saint's relics. The crowds outside would try to jam themselves in, while those inside were so squashed that they could not move. On occasions panic ensued and pilgrims were crushed underfoot, and it was not unknown for the monastic guardians of the shrine to be forced to take up the relics and scramble to safety through a window. At St Peter's in Rome, one of the most important relics was the sudarium of St Veronica (often known simply as the Veronica). This cloth was said to have been miraculously imprinted with the features of Jesus after Veronica gave it to him to wipe his face, as he walked towards his place of execution. When this cloth was displayed in the Jubilee Year of 1300 such huge crowds surged forward to see it that some were injured in the crush. One of the recorded victims was an English pilgrim named William of Derby, whose leg was smashed and who died shortly afterwards.

On less crowded occasions pilgrims could be safely guided around the shrine and its stations by authorized guides, who doubtless persuaded them of the spiritual benefit of donating money or other gifts such as rings, brooches and pins, at the principal shrine and the various altars. Pilgrims' offerings were often the mainstay of a shrine's upkeep. They could range from paupers' pennies to a rich man's donation of gold, silver and gemstones; they could include livestock such as chickens and geese and commodities such as wax, cheese and oil. King Louis VII of France donated an annual gift to the monks of Canterbury of 100 barrels of wine from his personal cellars, granted in perpetuity.

In addition to leaving donations, pilgrims also left votive offerings, often cast in wax or made of wood or silver, that represented the nature of their illness or condition from which they hoped to be cured (or had been cured) by the intervention of the saint. For example, a Frenchman from Montpellier who had successfully prayed to the Virgin Mary for the recovery of two missing oxen took two wax miniatures of the beasts to the Church of Our Lady at Rocamadour as a token of his thanks. An assortment of votive objects could be seen at shrines, such as crutches, prisoners' iron

Modern votive offerings at the fourteenth-century Pandanassa Monastery in Mystras, Greece, perform the same function as those in medieval times.

shackles and paintings showing the pilgrims or the miracles they had received. Models of eyes, teeth, arms and ears – usually on sale outside the shrine – would signify the healing of those parts of the body, while a model ship or anchor might betoken being saved from a shipwreck. At Exeter Cathedral, wax models left at the tomb of the local saint Edmund Lacy included horses' legs. Another custom was to leave a candle of the same height as the person who needed healing. The thread used to measure the height of the invalid was often made into the candle wick and if the person was very tall it was first wound into a coil, or 'trindle', before being set in the wax.

Before leaving the shrine for the journey home, pilgrims might take away holy water which had touched the saint's relics, or dust from his tomb; or if they had gone to a shrine for penitential reasons, they would obtain a certificate from a sacristan to prove that they had visited it. Another common practice was purchasing the shrine's badge or, as it was called, 'sign', which was usually made of tin, pewter, brass or lead and was often perforated. Pinned onto hats and cloaks, these badges were not only souvenirs of the journey – like the exotic passport stamps of modern travellers – but also showed that the person in question was a bona fide pilgrim.

The best-known badge was the scallop shell, at first associated only with Santiago de Compostela but later so popular that it came to signify pilgrimage in general. In the Holy Land pilgrims could buy a palm leaf to take home (the surname 'Palmer' comes from this practice), while in Rome there were two main badges: one showed St Peter and St Paul with a key and a sword; the other was the vernicle, a representation of the Veronica, which came in the form of either a badge or a small cloth. In the fourteenth-century allegorical poem by William Langland, the pilgrim Piers Plowman is described bearing on his hat a 'hundred small phials' and shell badges from Compostela; he also had the sign of the cross on his cloak, along with a token of the keys of Rome and a vernicle pinned to his chest. In Amiens badges showed the head of John the Baptist, in Rocamadour the Virgin Mary, and in Cologne

ABOVE: Lead pilgrim badges from the shrine of St Thomas at Canturbury Cathedral. One shows the saint aboard a ship, the other his head and archbishop's mitre.

the Magi, whose remains were reputedly enshrined there. Canterbury had a number of different signs. Most showed St Thomas – whether riding a horse, sitting on his archiepiscopal throne, on board a ship or standing above a peacock. Another popular Canterbury badge showed the ampulla, the lead flask used by pilgrims to take back 'Canterbury water', an efficacious brew made from water mixed with drops of St Thomas's blood.

The manufacture and selling of badges was a lucrative business and monopolies were granted by the popes to produce them. In 1199 Innocent III gave the canons of St Peter's in Rome the sole right to make and sell badges relating to their church; and in 1207 the same pope tried to stop unauthorized badge-sellers plying their trade in Spain along the road to Compostela. The fact that subsequent popes tried to halt this practice on another four occasions during the thirteenth century indicates that badge-sellers were a determined breed. In Rocamadour the right to sell badges was shared by the Bishop of Tulle and the De Valon family, who also split the profits. Rocamadour locals, watching money change hands rapidly, decided to produce badges themselves – illegally – and for a while significantly cut into the profits of the licensed traders.

Badges were also believed to be receptacles of spiritual power. Pilgrims would press them onto the shrine's holy relics in order to absorb their 'spiritual energy', which it was believed would give physical protection against malefactors on the return journey. Back home the badges were often fixed to the sides of houses, cattle-sheds and wells, or buried in fields, so that they could work their positive influence. The French king Louis XI was so convinced of the power of badges that he festooned his hat with them and would kiss them at every opportunity, especially when receiving good or bad news.

ROME

Rome's enduring prestige for Christians down the centuries was founded on two main historical reasons. Firstly, it had more saints and martyrs to honour than any other city, including the two greatest apostles, St Peter and St Paul, who according to tradition were executed (probably in about AD 64 during the reign of Nero) and laid to rest there. Secondly, in the Middle Ages, the city's classical status as 'mistress of the world' and its grandiose monuments, even in their delapidation, still inspired awe. As the twelfth-century French bishop Hildebert of Lavardin wrote in a poem: 'Nothing matches you, O Rome, although you are in ruin/Your broken buildings show how great you were in former times.' But the attraction of Rome for pilgrims fluctuated, its popularity influenced by the ever-shifting prestige of the papacy and the political stability of Italy. Feuding between rival city states as well as between the pope and the Holy Roman Emperor frequently led to wars that devastated the countryside and spawned outlaws, robbers and condottieri. The 900s and 1200s were particularly turbulent times. In the fourteenth century an anonymous Rome-bound English

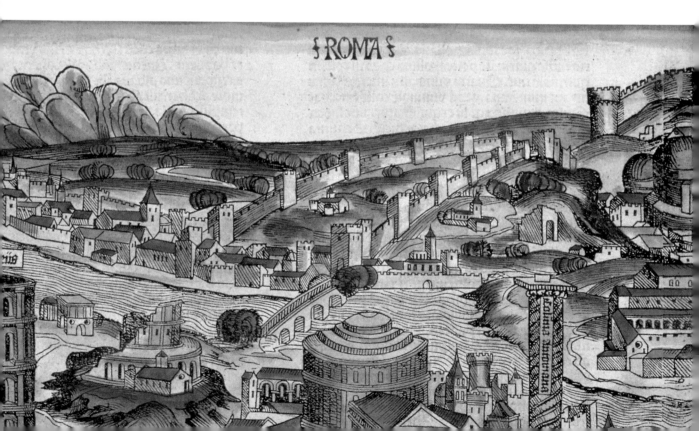

ROMA

pilgrim recorded that there had recently been a war which had involved no less than twelve cities: Milan, Pavia, Piacenza, Cremona, Mantua, Bobbio, Padua, Florence, Bologna, Reggio, Modena and Pisa.

Physical conditions in Rome itself could also deter pilgrims. In summer it was often unbearably hot, with malaria common. One thirteenth-century cleric described the city as being infested with mosquitoes and scorpions. The fifteenth-century chronicler Adam of Usk lamented how the Rome that had once been a city of nobles and palaces was now a place of shacks, robbers, wolves and vermin. Nevertheless, even when its fortunes were at a nadir during the 1300s, when the popes were residing in Avignon during the period known as the 'Babylonian Captivity' (an ironic reference to the Jews' exile in Babylon), Rome still attracted a stream of pilgrims. This was particularly so in the Jubilee Years of 1300, 1350 and

A panoramic view of the city of Rome from the *Nuremberg Chronicle*, a vast pictorial history of the world from its creation up to the 1490s.

1390, when by papal decree plenary indulgences were granted to those who visited the city and its shrines (see pages 96–7).

The main motive for making a pilgrimage to Rome was less likely to be to seek a cure for sickness as to gain absolution from sin and to smooth the path to heaven in the afterlife – for who would facilitate this better than the city's greatest saint, Peter the gatekeeper of heaven? The English scholar Alcuin, Charlemagne's spiritual mentor, said that people went to Rome 'either to mourn their sins with the greater outpouring of their faith in the presence of the blessed apostles, or to prepare with more abounding hope to open the way to celestial life'. In early medieval times those who travelled with these hopes included bishops, monks and even kings such as the Anglo-Saxon Wessex kings Caedwalla and Ine who, according to the later medieval chronicler Matthew Paris, founded a hostel in Rome, known as the Schola Saxonum, for the benefit of English pilgrims. Other nations, including the Franks, Lombards and Frisians, also established their own hostels. These institutions probably evolved into mini-communities of expatriates, to which some pilgrims came to live out the rest of their lives.

From western Europe there were several main routes to Rome, all of them converging at the Alps, which were traversed usually by the Simplon, Mount Cenis or Great St Bernard passes. The Alps posed a constant hazard to pilgrims. The ice was treacherous, the avalanches frequent and the vertiginous heights terrifying – Adam of Usk had to blindfold himself as he was borne over them in an ox-wagon. They were also bitterly cold. When John of Canterbury reached for his ink-bottle on the Great St Bernard Pass in 1188 he found its contents a frozen mass. His beard was shaggy with ice and his breath 'congealed in a long icicle'. But at least the Alps did not freeze him to death, a fate that befell Aelfsige, Archbishop of Canterbury, in 959.

A miniature plan of the city of Rome (c. 1415–16) by the Limburg brothers, showing the large number of churches and shrines to be visited by the medieval pilgrim.

One of the more detailed surviving pilgrim itineraries to Rome is that of an Icelandic monk named Nicholas of Munkathvera, from Iceland to Rome in the mid-twelfth century. After sailing from Iceland to Norway, Nicholas made his way to Denmark then travelled almost due south through Germany. On the way he stopped at Minden, Mainz, Worms, Speyer and Strasbourg. He proceeded to Basle in Switzerland then on to the Great St Bernard Pass, more than 8,000 feet above sea level. Covered in snow for nine months of the year, the Pass was famous for its hospice, founded by St Bernard of Menthon in 962. Once in Italy, Nicholas travelled across the fertile plain of Lombardy via Pavia and Piacenza, thence to Lucca, where he could have seen the famous Volto Santo, a venerable wooden crucifix said to have protective powers that locals believed could be transferred to the countless facsimiles they made of it. From Lucca he proceeded south, stopping at Siena, Viterbo and Sutri before entering Rome.

For medieval pilgrims, Rome offered an embarrassment of churches, shrines and relics. From the seventh century there were written 'pilgrim guides' describing circuits of the city that included a variety of catacombs, churches and shrines, climaxing with St Peter's Church. From the mid-eighth century martyrs' relics were transferred from the catacombs outside the city to churches within, and these became the goals of pilgrims. By the time Sigeric, Archbishop of Canterbury, was in Rome in 990 there were at least twenty-three churches to visit, which Sigeric accomplished in two days. Over the course of time, however, seven churches gained precedence over the others: those of St Mary the Greater, St Paul, St John Lateran, St Peter, St Cross, St Lawrence and St Sebastian. In the later Middle Ages it became necessary to visit all seven of these to gain a plenary indulgence. The first four were major basilicas in their own right. St Mary the Greater, which preserved a fragment of Jesus' manger, dated from the fourth and fifth centuries. According to legend, Pope Liberius (352–66) was shown which part of the Esquiline Hill he should build the church through the Virgin's footprints appearing in a miraculous fall of snow that covered the hilltop at the height of summer. The anniversary of the miracle, 5 August, is still commemorated by a 'snowfall' of white petals dropped from above inside the church.

St Paul's lay about one and a half miles south of the city walls and was founded by Constantine in 324, being enlarged later in the same century (it was completely rebuilt in the nineteenth century after a disastrous fire). Somewhat isolated from the daily concourse of the city and without the protection of its walls, St Paul's was liable to suffer neglect – as in the eleventh century, when sheep belonging to a local farmer used to wander into the nave. Matters improved in 1070 when a wealthy family of Amalfi presented the church with a pair of magnificent Byzantine bronze doors. St Paul's was the largest church in Christendom before St Peter's was rebuilt in the sixteenth century, and as it covered the tomb of the apostle it was a prime destination for pilgrims. William of Ventura recorded that in the Jubilee Year of 1300 so many pilgrims visited the church that two clerics worked round the clock at the high altar to gather in with rakes the mounds of coins left there.

St John Lateran, as was the case with St Cross, had once been a pagan Roman palace. It was the residence of the popes from the fourth century until the early fourteenth century. The church (which was rebuilt after a fire in the fourteenth century) was the home of several important relics and was considered a rival to St Peter's. Some relics, such as earth from the tomb of St John the Evangelist, must have seemed relatively mundane. Others, such as the rod of Aaron, bottles of blood and water from the side of the crucified Christ, and the five loaves and two fishes would surely have had a more profound imaginative appeal. The most famous relic was a full-length picture of Christ known as the 'Acheropita' (Greek for 'not created by human hands') because it was believed to have been painted by divine agency. Until the 1500s, on the Feast of the Assumption in August, the image was taken to St Mary the Greater in a procession that stopped in several places so that Christ's feet could be washed with herb-scented water.

Rome's greatest church, however, was St Peter's, built in the fourth century by Constantine I on Vatican Hill, over what was believed to be the tomb or cenotaph of the apostle. In 1939 archaeologists found dramatic support for this tradition when, excavating below the church's high altar, they found a small shrine dating back to the mid-second century AD. In the shrine were pieces of bone which in 1965 Pope Pius VI declared to be the mortal remains of St Peter, although many still doubt whether

A sixteenth-century fresco by Domenico Tasselli, showing how the interior of St Peter's looked before the church's reconstruction in the Renaissance.

such an identification can be justified. Nevertheless, it is clear that when Constantine built the church he chose the site of an important Christian shrine that had been venerated for more than 150 years.

An indication of what early pilgrims did when visiting St Peter's is given by St Gregory of Tours, who described the visit there of a churchman named Agiulf in about 590. Gregory wrote that the saint's shrine had a small window through which people poked their heads to make a petition to him. The custom was to let down at the same time a *brandea*, or strip of cloth. If this weighed more after it had been retracted, the prayer had been successful, the *brandea* having absorbed some of the saint's 'virtue'. Until the early 1500s, St Peter's retained the basic shape of its original rectangular exterior, but evolved inside with the addition of a crypt and various altars and treasures, including from the 700s onwards the Veronica, which in the fourteenth century became St Peter's main pilgrim attraction. The church was inspiring in its size and sumptuousness. An anonymous fourteenth-century English pilgrim was awestruck by its 'five roofs and four rows of columns' and the fact that the building was 'as long as a crossbow will shoot'. Outside, on the steps leading up to the church, small stalls sold fruit, bread, fish, vegetables and other foodstuffs, and other services provided included those of a dentist and a cobbler.

After the comparatively meagre years of the twelfth century, Rome experienced an increase in pilgrimage. This was partly due to the loss of the Crusader states in Palestine to Muslim armies – Jerusalem fell in 1244 – which encouraged pilgrims to go elsewhere, but also because Pope Innocent III and his successors improved facilities for pilgrims, created badges to rival those of other shrines, and increased the number of indulgences that could be obtained. Pilgrims swelled the native population by tens of thousands during Jubilee, or Holy, Years. The Christian Jubilee was probably suggested by the idea of a Hebrew holy year, described in Leviticus, which was to take place every fifty years and be a time of rest and peaceful accord. Pope Boniface VIII instituted the first Christian Jubilee Year in 1300, declaring that pilgrims who came to Rome stood to gain a plenary indulgence. The incentive worked, and contemporary estimates of the numbers visiting Rome that year varied between 200,000 and two million. One witness compared the incoming crowds to a swarm of ants or the dense lines of an army. Dante alluded in his *Inferno* to the crowds as well as to the one-way system enforced on the bridge of Sant'Angelo to ease congestion.

The second Jubilee year, in 1350, was also a papal triumph, although Rome had recently suffered from a serious earthquake and large swathes of Europe were devastated by the Black Death and the incessant warfare between England and France. Subsequent Jubilees, held at varying intervals, continued to draw large numbers. The sixth one, in 1450, was the occasion of a tragic accident on the bridge of Sant' Angelo. A panic-stricken mule created an uproar among the dense crowd of pedestrians resulting in scores of people being crushed or drowned in the Tiber. Few pilgrims made the journey to the seventh holy year in 1475 (the interval between Jubilees was now fixed at twenty-five years), but those who did were able to cross a new bridge, the Ponte Sisto, built to syphon off some of the crowds from Sant' Angelo.

It is not clear how many visitors in 1500 – the last Jubilee before the Reformation – were aware of the corruption of the astute but self-serving Pope Alexander VI, who, as Roderigo Borgia, had bribed his way to the pontificate; and it is difficult to judge whether negative opinions of the papacy tarred Rome's status as a place of pilgrimage with the same brush. Most simple, uneducated pilgrims no doubt arrived, worshipped, prayed, collected their indulgences, bought souvenirs and left Rome without much knowledge of, or concern for, papal or Church corruption. But others did care, and saw Alexander as the epitome of the Church's woes and Rome as their epicentre. One of the most vociferous critics was the Florentine reformer Savonarola, who railed against the decadence of the 'prostitute Church'. He was excommunicated by the pope and then executed in 1498 by his fellow citizens, sickened by his ultra-ascetic morality. There were others. Erasmus used satire to expose what he saw as Church iniquities; and in 1517 the German monk Martin Luther famously attacked the sale of indulgences intended by Pope Leo X to raise money to continue the renovation of St Peter's. While Rome's greatest building awaited fresh funds, the edifice of the Church began to tremble as the voices of Reform grew louder.

SANTIAGO DE COMPOSTELA

The pilgrimage to the cathedral shrine of Santiago de Compostela – home of the body of St James the Apostle – in Galicia, northwest Spain, was the greatest in medieval Christendom after those to Rome and Jerusalem. At the height of its popularity in the late eleventh and twelfth centuries, an estimated half a million pilgrims a year walked the paths and roads that led across the Pyrenees and the sun-burnt, wind-swept plains of the *meseta* to the misty mountains of Galicia, and onward to the shrine. Compostela's pilgrim badge, the scallop shell, was so ubiquitous that it became the symbol of pilgrimage in general. Dante, writing in his *La Vita Nuova* in 1292, defined 'pilgrim' in two ways – as someone who had left his place of birth and, more specifically, as someone who had journeyed to Compostela.

How St James became Spain's national saint and, indeed, how his body reached Galicia remain something of a mystery. Although the English monk Aldhelm recorded in 700 that St James had preached in Spain, there is no mention of this in early Christian texts or in the New Testament. What can be gleaned from the Gospels is that James, along with his brother John, was one of Jesus' closest disciples and was termed 'the Greater' to distinguish him from another apostle of the same name. Born in Galilee, a region whose people were renowned for being independent and spirited, James and John were the sons of Zebedee and nicknamed 'Boanerges' ('Sons of Thunder') because of their volcanic tempers.

The New Testament remains mostly silent about James's life after Jesus' crucifixion in about AD 33, except to note in the Acts of the Apostles (12:2) that he was martyred in Judea in AD 44 by King Herod Agrippa I. So how did his body arrive in Galicia, and how did his cult begin? Medieval legends present the answers to these questions in two distinct phases: the first deals with the miraculous transportation and burial of the apostle just after his martyrdom, the second with the equally miraculous discovery of his body hundreds of years later.

After James's death, according to the thirteenth-century compilation of saints' lives

The statue of St James the Apostle in the crown portal of the cathedral at Santiago de Compostela. He is shown dressed as a pilgrim, carrying a staff and wearing a broad-brimmed hat. Scallop shells adorn his hat and cloak.

known as *The Golden Legend*, two of his disciples carried his corpse to Jaffa, where they found a boat 'without a rudder or steersman'. These impediments notwithstanding, they put to sea and let God guide the vessel: the boat was duly blown westwards through the Pillars of Hercules (the Strait of Gibraltar), then northwards to a landfall on the Galician coast at the Roman settlement of Iria Flavia. The ruler of that area was a wily pagan queen named Lupa ('She-wolf') who, after creating obstacles for the disciples, finally allowed the apostle's body to be buried in the middle of her palace, which she turned into a church, having accepted the Christian faith herself.

The second scene of the story, which has a greater sense of historical truth, is set some 800 years after the apostolic era. The circumstances have radically changed. Galicia is now a Christian enclave in a Spain dominated by the Moors – the Muslim Arabs and Berbers who crossed from North Africa in 711 and conquered most of the Iberian peninsula. In 813, it is said, during the reign of the Christian King Alfonso II, who had managed to cling on to the far northwest of Spain, a hermit named Pelagius was guided Magi-like by a celestial light to a field in which he discovered a stone tomb. The local bishop inspected the bones in the tomb, identified them as the remains of St James and alerted Alfonso, who arrived post-haste. Perhaps realizing the potential of such a momentous discovery, the king immediately adopted James as his patron saint and had a new church built on his burial site. This became known as Compostela (the first written record of the name occurs in a document of 912), a word that was popularly thought to derive from the Latin *campus*, a 'field', and *stella*, a 'star', and to refer to the celestial light that led to the saint being discovered. The truth may be more prosaic. Modern etymologists think the name comes from the Latin *compostum*, a 'cemetery', or possibly from *composta*, meaning 'established' and referring to the city's first stronghold.

At a time when the movement for the reconquest of Spain from its Moorish rulers was nascent, the tenacious faith and sometimes all-too-human aggression that James displays in the Gospel stories made him an ideal patron saint of Compostela and Spain. This was fully borne out two years after the death of Alfonso, at the battle of Clavijo in 842. The Spanish under Ramiro I faced annihilation by Abdurrahman II and his huge Moorish army, but when all seemed lost St James is said to have appeared in the sky as a knight on a white charger and galvanized the Spanish troops into routing the enemy. In the Spanish psyche, the Son of Thunder of the Gospels easily slipped into his new identity as a crusading warrior saint, and was soon represented as Santiago Matamoros – the 'Moor Killer', mounted on a horse and wielding a sword.

What is especially interesting about the story of how St James came to Spain is the way it echoes the Irish *peregrinatio*: the aimless wandering across land and sea for the love of Christ. This is exactly what James's disciples do – committing themselves to a boat and trusting in God's providence to guide them to the right destination. Was the writer of *The Golden Legend* influenced by tales of the early medieval Irish pilgrim saints, which he combined with other stories that linked James with Spain? It is also interesting that the legends are reminiscent of the archetypal myth of the 'sleeping hero', in which a legendary national figure such as King Arthur or King Holger the Dane defies death and lies sleeping in a cave, ready to wake up when his country needs him. Although James did actually die, the way in which his body goes missing for centuries and is then rediscovered at a time of national crisis, inspiring his followers to snatch victory from the jaws of defeat, has a similar mythic pattern to it.

As news of the rediscovery of St James and his efficacy as a divine warrior filtered across Europe, pilgrims began to make their way to Compostela in increasing numbers. The first documented foreign pilgrim was Godescalc, the bishop of Le Puy, who led a group of followers there in about 950. In the next century Compostela grew more prosperous as the great French monastery of Cluny drew it into its orbit. Perceiving that Compostela and its warrior saint were crucial factors in the fight against the infidel, the Cluniacs built hospitals, priories and bridges to facilitate the passage of pilgrims to the shrine. Its prestige was further enhanced in 1078 with the building of a new cathedral in the Romanesque style of the time, with an ambulatory at the east end to enable more pilgrims to walk around the high altar (the building was completed in the early thirteenth century and given a virtuoso Baroque facade in the eighteenth century). Four main pilgrim routes to Compostela became established in France, starting from Tours, Vézelay, Le Puy and Arles, which acted as assembly points. The routes headed southwest to the Pyrenees, which they traversed via two passes. Once in Spain they combined to form one main route known as the Camino Francés, the French Way, which medieval travellers imagined to be reflected at night in the silvery stellar trail of the Milky Way (which they nicknamed the Way of St James, just as pilgrims to Walsingham called it the Walsingham Way).

Compostela's prestige was maintained during the twelfth century mainly through the efforts of its dynamic bishop Diego Gelmírez, who continued work on the cathedral and built a pilgrim hospice and an aqueduct. He also managed to obtain privileges from the pope, notably the elevation of the bishopric to metropolitan status in 1124. Evidence of the popularity of the Compostela pilgrimage at this time comes not only from material remains found on the pilgrim roads but also from what has been described as medieval Europe's first travel guidebook, a text that appears in a manuscript known as the *Codex Calixtinus*. This work, comprising a number of books, is thought to have been edited, and perhaps partially written, in about the 1140s by a French monk from Poitou named Aimery Picaud. The *Codex*'s fifth book, known as the *Pilgrim's Guide*, vividly describes the routes and conditions of the Compostela pilgrimage, and the various people, customs, food, places to stay, relics and hazards likely to be encountered during the journey. The *Pilgrim's Guide* can be brutally frank, especially in its description of local peoples. While the men of Poitou, it assures us, are handsome, spirited, generous and make brave, skilful soldiers, the people of Bordeaux are criticized for their coarse speech, though their wine is – not surprisingly – considered excellent, as is their fish. Further south, the Gascons are branded as poor, greedy, coarse and garrulous, though the book does concede that they are good fighters and hospitable – but what a shame that they tend to drink from the same cup and dress so shabbily! The Basques, whose country straddled the Pyrenees, are lambasted as a fierce people who speak a barbarous language and extort money from pilgrims; and the people of Navarre in Spain are stigmatized as perfidious drunks addicted to robbing and murdering.

The *Pilgrim's Guide* divides the 500-mile route through Spain itself into thirteen stages, starting from Roncesvalles in the Pyrenees. Yet it is misleading to think in terms of one unique path from which pilgrims did not stray. Many English pilgrims preferred to sail directly to northwest Spain and make a relatively short overland trip to the shrine. And although pilgrims on the Camino Francés would have followed the same route for a large part of the journey, they would also inevitably deviate to other paths – perhaps to visit a local shrine, to take a short-cut, to avoid a rumoured troubled spot, or to make a detour around a broken bridge or flooded road.

From Roncesvalles, pilgrims headed southwest towards Pamplona and the town of Estella, nestling below a gorge, which according to the *Pilgrim's Guide* produced fine wine, fish, meat and bread. Continuing west to Burgos, they passed through Villafranca, founded (as its name suggests) by French pilgrims in the 1100s. From here the route entered the *meseta*, continuing to Léon and across to Astorga. From this point onwards travellers experienced a change of scenery as foothills and mountains loomed before them, and the enticing prospect of misty, green Galicia beckoned beyond. Climbing a few miles beyond Rabanal, travellers came to the town of Foncebadon, 5,000 feet above sea level, where they would add a stone to the cairn, which still exists. From here the way ran down the western slopes of the mountains to Pontferrada, site of a still-surviving fairytale castle built by the Knights Templar in 1119, and Villafranca de Bierzo – another town founded by the French in the eleventh century. Here, at the local church's Gate of the Pardon, pilgrims who were physically unable to manage the rest of the journey were granted the indulgence they would have received at Compostela. About thirty miles farther on pilgrims at last entered Galicia, at the town of Cebreiro, and continued through Triacastella – where it was customary to pick up pieces of limestone to be burnt to make much-needed building mortar in Compostela – to Portomarin.

The next main destination was Palas do Rei – the *Pilgrim Guide's* penultimate stop – which used to be the capital of the kings of the Visigoths, who ruled Spain between the fall of Rome and the Muslim conquest. Thirty miles to the west lay Arzua, the last town of any size before Compostela itself, a further forty-five miles away. Just before

ABOVE: The tiny thirteenth-century Romanesque hermitage of San Miguel outside Poblición de Campos in northern Spain, one of the stopping places on the pilgrim route to Santiago de Compostela.

Compostela, at the village of San Marcos, pilgrims would climb the hill of Monte del Gozo to catch their first glimpse of the cathedral and its nine soaring medieval towers (now vanished, bar one) and to add a stone to the cairn there, thus earning a hundred days off their stint in purgatory.

In Compostela itself, pilgrims made their way to the cathedral square, where they could buy scallop shells and various items of kit such as shoes, belts and scrips, as well as medicinal herbs. There they could refresh themselves in the magnificent fountain with its bronze column topped by four lions, who spewed water from their mouths into a basin big enough to hold fifteen people. All that remained to do then was to enter the cathedral's vast interior through its magnificent carved doorways. The building, the *Pilgrim's Guide* says, measured 'fifty-three times the height of a man' in length (about 300 feet), and was filled with stone and white marble columns carved with flowers, birds, animals, humans and biblical scenes. It had two storeys, 'like a royal palace', and its upper galleries contained three of the cathedral's fourteen altars. At the east end, three large silver lamps hung in front of the altar of St James, their flickering light playing on the altar's frontal, or decorative hanging, which was embroidered with gold and silver.

After pilgrims had toured the nave, the transepts and the ambulatory at the far east end, their devotions reached a climax with the descent into the gloom of the crypt to touch, kiss and pray at St James's tomb. This, according to the *Pilgrim's Guide*, was 'lit by the otherworldly gleam of carbuncles, honoured without cease by heavenly fragrances, bathed in the glow of celestial candles and watched over by attendant angels'. Having visited the tomb the pilgrims were, at long last, allowed to receive their indulgence for the pilgrimage. After that they could visit other churches and the rest of the city, before contemplating the long, difficult journey home. Many would return with a new perspective on life – that is if the *Codex Calixtinus* is to be believed, claiming as it does that 'he who enters Santiago sad, will leave it happy'.

The baroque towers of the cathedral loom over the large and thriving town of Santiago de Compostela, which has grown around the shrine of St James there.

CANTERBURY

When Thomas Becket became Archbishop of Canterbury in 1162, during the reign of Henry II, the fame of Canterbury Cathedral was not due to the fact that it was a place of pilgrimage but because it was the spiritual centre of English Christianity, the home of archbishops of the English Church since the time of the missionary saint Augustine at the end of the sixth century. After Becket's assassination by four of Henry's knights on 29 December 1170 and his canonization three years later, Canterbury became one of the major pilgrim destinations of medieval Christendom, along with Santiago de Compostela, Rome and Jerusalem. Tertullian had written that the blood of martyrs was the seed of the church: with Becket's blood Canterbury grew into a flourishing pilgrim shrine almost literally overnight. For 350 years, until the Reformation, pilgrims converged on the cathedral 'from every shire's end of England', as Chaucer wrote, and from all over continental Europe.

What is interesting about Canterbury is that its birth, growth, decline and death as a place of pilgrimage is relatively well defined and documented, beginning with Becket's martyrdom and ending with the Protestant Reformers' destruction of the shrine in the sixteenth century. That is not to say it did not attract a misty film of pious legends also. Reports of miracles connected with the shrine and the intercession of 'St Thomas of Canterbury' were legion. Contemporary reports claim that the saint appeared in visions and that through him the blind saw, the deaf heard and the crooked were made straight. Drops of his blood were added to the cathedral's well to produce a unique elixir with which pilgrims eagerly filled their lead flasks, or ampullas. Emperors and kings paid homage to him, including Henry II, who in 1174 walked barefoot to the shrine in a public show of penitence and allowed himself to be scourged by the monks there; and even Henry VIII, who prayed at the shrine only a few years before his self-serving state policies resulted in its demise. St Thomas's shrine not only radiated spiritual power but also possessed great material wealth, from the coins of peasants to the gold and silver plates, cups, brooches and gems of the wealthy. According to Erasmus, who visited the shrine in about 1514, 'gold was the meanest

The great central tower of Canterbury Cathedral at dusk. The tower was completed in about 1495 and is 235 feet high, making it visible for many miles around.

thing to be seen there . . . some [jewels] were larger than the egg of a goose'. Most spectacular, perhaps, was the gift of Louis VII, who in 1179 presented an enormous ruby – 'le Régale de France' – which was fated to end up set in a ring gracing the hand of Henry VIII. When Henry's men carried off the shrine's wealth in 1538 they needed twenty-six wagons to do the job.

Canterbury is inextricably tied up with the compelling life story of Becket, who had the ability to reinvent himself so radically. The Chancellor who had upheld the power of the state against the Church became the implacable defender of ecclesiastical rights; the worldly lord, fastidious in his choice of food and wine, became an austere churchman revelling in asceticism (when the Canterbury monks examined his dead body they found beneath his robes a hair shirt seething with lice). Despite justified charges of pride, obstinacy and ostentation, Becket still emerges as a rock of principle from the swirling waters of corruption and wheeler-dealing in twelfth-century Church and state politics. His willpower, self-conviction and loyalty – whether to the Church or the king – as well as his dignified bearing and charisma made him as popular with the common people as it did a marked man among envious fellow clerics and avaricious nobles.

Becket was born in London in 1118, the son of a wealthy Anglo-Norman merchant. In his mid-twenties he joined the household of Theobald, Archbishop of Canterbury, who was so impressed by his charm, energy and all-round competence that he had no hesitation in recommending him to Henry II for the post of Chancellor, one of the most important posts in the country. Not only did Becket perform his new tasks with efficiency and brio, he also formed a close friendship with Henry, to the extent that Theobald remarked in a letter to him that in popular opinion 'you and the king are one heart and one mind'. When Theobald died in 1161, Henry must have seen a heaven-sent opportunity to appoint Becket as the new Archbishop of Canterbury and through him wield greater influence over the Church. For some time the relationship between Crown and Church had been vexed, with both parties seeking to extend or consolidate their spheres of interest, which were often mutually exclusive. One major sticking point was the right of the Church to try churchmen charged with breaking the law in ecclesiastical courts – where punishments were relatively lenient – and not in civil courts.

Henry, a volatile, headstrong man, prone to violent fits of temper, was determined to bring the Church to heel on this and other matters; and now he had the chance to install his own man, his boon companion, at the top of the clerical pyramid. Despite Becket's reluctance and forebodings, Henry had him ordained a priest, consecrated as a bishop and enthroned as archbishop in the space of thirty-six hours. But any sense of triumphal expectation Henry might have had soon drained away as he watched in bemused horror as Becket transferred his immense talents and loyalty to another, heavenly, master – and took up the Church's cause.

The king and archbishop, equally matched, made moves and countermoves like chess grandmasters, each trying to rally support, exert pressure and gain advantage for his cause. Then in 1164, feeling the full force of the king's frustrated anger, Becket decided it would be prudent to flee to France. There he remained until 1170 when a partial *rapprochement* with Henry enabled him to return to England and a hero's welcome from the common people. But the modicum of renewed goodwill between the two men evaporated when Becket openly denounced the two bishops who, during his exile, had officiated at the crowning of Henry's young son as co-regent – contrary to canon law.

When news of this latest defiance reached Henry, on campaign in France, he is said to have shouted, 'Will no one rid me of this low-born priest?' The question may have been rhetorical. But four of his knights, FitzUrse, de Tracy, Brito and de Moreville, took Henry at his word. On reaching Canterbury they forced a confrontation with Becket, who, realizing their intention and seemingly resigned to matyrdom, refused to flee or to admit their charges of treason. Cajoled by his fretting monks, Becket took

ABOVE: An example from one of the spectacular thirteenth-century series of 'miracle windows' in the Trinity Chapel, Canterbury Cathedral, depicting miraculous cures effected postumously by St Thomas.

109

refuge in the cathedral but refused to let them bar the door, declaring that they should not make 'a fortress of the house of God; by suffering rather than by fighting we shall triumph over the enemy'. The four knights followed him and, careless of the sanctity of the place, struggled with the archbishop and cut him down, slicing off a piece of his skull in the process. They then raided the archbishop's palace for valuables and rode off into a night of torrential rain.

While Christendom reacted with shock and outrage to what Pope Alexander III called 'this most monstrous crime', and Henry received the news of his erstwhile friend's death with what appeared to be genuine grief (he fasted for three days on milk

and almonds), the cult of Thomas Becket was born. The first 'miracle' happened on the night after the murder, when a local knight claimed to have cured his paralysed wife with a cloth he had dipped into Becket's spilt blood. A few days later a Gloucester woman claimed to have been cured of severe headaches after praying to Becket; and a Berkshire knight attributed to his intercession the cure of his damaged arm. Other miracles quickly followed and during the first decade after Becket's death more than 700 were recorded by two contemporary monks, Benedict and William.

In the early thirteenth century, some of the miracles were depicted in the cathedral's stained glass and can still be seen today. They show, for example, how a workman, accidentally buried alive while laying drainage pipes, was extricated from the ground; and how a monk was cured of skin disease, a forester of an arrow wound, and a carpenter of a leg injury. News of miracles such as these spread through Europe, as did relics of Becket, including pieces of his clothing and vestments, and domestic utensils. Hymns and commemorative services in his honour echoed around countless churches across the continent, and murals, stained-glass windows, carved roof bosses and medals were made depicting his final moments. With the growth of his cult and his fame as a miracle worker, it was only a matter of time before Alexander III canonized Becket: he did so on 21 February 1173.

At first the saint's tomb lay in the crypt of the cathedral and consisted of a coffin enclosed by a rectangular marble chest. This had two holes on each side to enable pilgrims to reach in and touch the coffin itself. On one occasion an agile madman squeezed himself through one of these holes into the space between the chest and the coffin and managed to scramble out just as the monks were contemplating having to smash the tomb to liberate him. Pilgrims made their way to the tomb after visiting the spot in the northwest transept where Becket had died, as well as the high altar, where his body had been laid out immediately after his death. In 1220, forty-six years after a fire destroyed part of the cathedral, the saint's remains were ceremonially translated to the newly completed Trinity Chapel and placed inside a gold-plated tomb. Hanging above was a gold-wire net on which pilgrims left gifts of devotion.

A fifteenth-century alabaster panel depicting the murder of
Thomas Becket in Canterbury Cathedral by knights of Henry II.

The same year saw the completion of the Corona Chapel, east of the tomb, which was built to house the severed fragment of Becket's skull, mounted in gold and set with jewels.

Apart from the great kings who made their way to St Thomas's shrine, the most famous visitors were probably the fictional creations of Geoffrey Chaucer, whose *Canterbury Tales* describes the journey of a group of pilgrims from London to Canterbury and the tales they recount to entertain each other along the way. Chaucer's characters give a good idea of the types of people who would have trekked to Canterbury in the late Middle Ages – a journey he himself probably made in 1386. They include a 'very perfect, gentle' knight; an urbane monk with a penchant for hunting, whose horse's bridle tinkled with tiny 'Canterbury bells'; a poor parson who was 'rich in holy thought and work'; a red-bearded miller who played the bagpipes; and a five-times married widow from Bath who was something of a pilgrimage addict, having gone to Jerusalem three times as well as Rome, Boulogne, Santiago de Compostela and Cologne.

Setting out from Southwark, pilgrims from London such as Chaucer's group would have travelled southeast along Watling Street to Greenwich, Dartford and then Rochester, where many visited the tomb of St William of Perth, a Scottish pilgrim who had been murdered near the town en route to the Holy Land. Farther on lay Sittingbourne, Faversham, where a Cluniac abbey housed a sliver of the True Cross, Boughton and Harbledown, where the Norman church of St Nicholas kept part of Becket's shoe, which pilgrims were invited to kiss. Just beyond Harbledown came the first glimpse of Canterbury Cathedral's two great towers 'that seem to salute the visitor from afar' as Erasmus noted in 1514. Inside the city, the poorer pilgrims would have sought out lodgings at monastic guest houses, while the wealthy repaired to inns and hostleries such as 'The Chequers', which still survives in its later Tudor incarnation. They would then make their way to the cathedral to be guided around the pilgrimage stations by the resident monks.

The site of Thomas Becket's martyrdom, in the northwest transept of Canterbury Cathedral, is marked by a simple inscription and a small altar. His shrine, however, was housed in the sumptuous Trinity Chapel at the east end of the cathedral.

The other main pilgrimage route was from Winchester, the principal assembly point for foreigners arriving at Southampton. From Winchester, having visited the cathedral's shrine of St Swithun, pilgrims headed east probably by way of Alton, Dorking and Aylesford, where some would have rested at the Carmelite friary, founded by St Simon Stock in the twelfth century. Farther east at Boxley they could have seen the famous Boxley Rood, or Crucifix. This wooden statue, which may have been originally designed for pageants, had a hidden mechanism that made its eyes and lips move – in the sixteenth century the Protestant Reformers were to claim that the statue reacted appropriately to the pilgrims' offerings: mere silver made it look vexed but gold apparently caused its 'jaws to wag merrily'. (The Reformers also exposed its 'engines and old wire' and eventually burnt it in public.) From Boxley the route passed through Charing, where the relic of John the Baptist's execution block could be seen in the local church, to the village of Chilham and from there beside the River Stour through woods to Canterbury.

St Thomas's shrine attracted a continual (although later diminishing) stream of pilgrims until the early sixteenth century. In 1220, when the saint's relics were translated to the choir, more than £1,100 had been gathered at the shrine; in 1535, three years before its dissolution, the total was £36. The cult was vulnerable to the late medieval trend of older saints being replaced in people's affections by more recent ones. This tendency was reflected in propagandic miracle stories, such as the one that told of a baby who swallowed a badge depicting St Thomas: efforts to remove the badge from the choking child failed until the name of Henry VI – who was murdered in 1471 and came to be viewed as a saint shortly afterwards – was invoked and the badge was duly regurgitated. So Thomas was already yesterday's saint when in 1538 Henry VIII violated his shrine and ordered him to be regarded as a 'rebel and traitor' rather than Chaucer's 'holy blissful martyr'. Yet though the king tried hard to extirpate St Thomas's cult – he ordered references to his name in prayer books to be excised and depictions of him in murals and windows obliterated – he could not sever the saint's association with the cathedral any more than he could erase his memory.

JERUSALEM AND THE HOLY LAND

'I cared never for eating, drinking nor sleeping; the hours of darkness which are appointed for men's rest were grievous to me; my bed was a thorn to me, my berth a hell. I could no longer read or write, or converse with men as before; but my only pleasure was to sit at the prow of the galley upon the horns thereof, and from thence to look ceaselessly across the wide sea, that by the toil of my eyes I might quiet the fever of my mind.' The words of the German friar Felix Fabri, who made two pilgrimages to Jerusalem in 1480 and 1483, capture the intensity of emotion medieval Western pilgrims could feel waiting for their first glimpse of the Holy Land on the horizon. Ever since Empress Helena 'discovered' in 326 the cross on which Jesus was crucified, Palestine had become the most prized of pilgrim destinations. No other place could compare with the land of Jesus' birth, mission, death and resurrection – which was also believed to be the location of the Second Coming.

With the conquests of the Crusaders from the end of the eleventh century, pilgrim traffic to the Holy Land received a new lease of life. One of those whose journeys were recorded at this time was a Russian monk named Daniel, who described the River Jordan in terms his brethren back home would understand – explaining that it was similar to the River Snov in the width of its mouth and occasional marshiness, but different in that it was the home of wild pigs, panthers and lions. Also travelling at that time was the Icelandic abbot Nicholas of Munkathvera (see page 93), who thought that Jórgalaborg (Jerusalem) was the 'most splendid of all cities'.

As the impetus of the Crusades petered out, Muslim armies gradually regained their hold of Palestine, with the last Crusader state falling in 1291. Even so, determined pilgrims still continued to make the journey there, increasingly by sea as the turbulent situation in eastern Europe and the decline of the Byzantine Empire, culminating in the fall of Constantinople to the Ottoman Turks in 1453, made the overland route steadily more perilous. The best, most convenient way to travel was in a Venetian ship. In the early thirteenth century Venice developed the first pilgrim 'package tours', with private shipowners, licensed by the state, providing transport, food and accommodation for a payment that also included local taxes and guides' fees. The state reserved the right to inspect ships and impose regulations for the comfort and safety of passengers. (Even so, unscrupulous Venetian captains sometimes tried to pack in

too many pilgrims, or cramped them by loading up the vessels with cargo to sell on their return home.) Another factor in favour of Venetian ships was that in the fifteenth century, when hostile Turkish and pirate ships roved around the eastern Mediterranean like sharks, Venetian navy patrols provided a degree of security.

The trials, tribulations – and moments of sublime joy – of the round trip from Venice to the Holy Land are described in detail by Felix Fabri in his *Evagatorium in Terrae Sanctae*, a colourful record of his two trips to Palestine and one of the best guides to the pilgrimage there. The value of the account lies in the fact that Felix combines a traditional medieval piety with a Renaissance-like curiosity about the world around him. Through him it is possible to experience both the interior life of the pilgrim as well as the novel sights and sounds of the journey. Although devout himself, he is able to distance himself from, and reflect upon, the more extreme expressions of pilgrim devotion and unquestioning belief in miracles that had been commonly found in earlier times. In short, it is possible to sense in Felix the medieval age transforming into the modern one. He does not, for example, deny the veracity of miracle stories, but he prefers a natural explanation if one exists. In the Church of the Holy Sepulchre, for example, he remarks upon six constantly dripping marble columns and mentions the popular tradition that the drops were the columns' 'tears', shed in sympathy with Jesus and the Virgin Mary. While acknowledging his respect for the 'opinion of the common people', Felix gives his own considered observation that the dripping was caused by a type of marble so cold that it condensed the air around it into water.

Felix's first expedition to Palestine in 1480 proved unsatisfactory, mainly because the Venetian captain in charge of the trip cut it short, leaving his charges only nine frenzied days in which to see the sights of Jerusalem – meagre rations after six weeks at sea. As soon as Felix arrived back in Italy he vowed to return to the Holy Land. In 1483 he fulfilled his oath, making the journey as a chaplain to four German noblemen. On 2 June, their Venetian trireme with its crew, galley slaves, and a motley group of pilgrims from France, Germany, England, Ireland, Hungary, Bohemia and elsewhere, set off to sea. After stops at Rovigno on the Croatian coast and Methone

The pivotal position of Jerusalem in medieval Christian thinking is reflected by the Psalter Map (*c.* 1250), which places the Holy City at the centre of the world.

in southwest Greece, they arrived at Crete, where the only available accommodation was a brothel. Luckily, the German proprietress, sensitive to the pilgrims' feelings, cleared the place and provided them with a delicious supper. From Crete the route took them to Rhodes and Cyprus, after which the pilgrims' anticipation of catching the first glimpse of their destination intensified. Finally, at sunrise on 1 July, the Holy Land was sighted – a moment celebrated by a joyful rendering of the *Te Deum*.

The pilgrims' excitement at arriving at Jaffa was soon checked by their reception by the Saracens, who laboriously registered the new arrivals, then lodged them in some nearby ruined vaults – which, as the pilgrims found to their disgust, the Saracens used as lavatories – until arrangements for their transfer to Jerusalem could be finalized. Eventually, on 8 July, the Saracens provided the pilgrims with donkeys. Felix employed the same friendly guide whom he had used on his first trip, and gave the man a pair of German iron stirrups – to his evident joy. Escorted by armed Saracens to protect them from opportunist Bedouin tribesmen, the pilgrims set off towards Jerusalem via the town of Ramle, where Father Paul, the prior of the Franciscan house in Jerusalem and chief representative of the Latin Church in Palestine, spelled out for them twenty-seven essential rules the pilgrims had to obey to stay out of trouble with their Saracen hosts. Formulated after years of practical experience, the rules included not stepping over Saracen graves, not laughing aloud in public, not gazing at Saracen women, not entering mosques and not retaliating to any provocation. Forewarned and forearmed, the group continued on their way until suddenly 'like a flash of lightning . . . Jerusalem shone forth'. Straightaway the pilgrims dismounted and bowed down to the earth and prayed. Then with 'eyes full of tears' and 'cheeks wet with joy' they resumed their journey with the priests and monks singing the *Te Deum*, but softly, so as not to rile the Saracen escort.

The pilgrims entered the city from the west by the Fish Gate (now called the Jaffa Gate) and were brought to the Church of the Holy Sepulchre which, one of the resident friars announced, was 'worshipped by the whole world'. At these words the pilgrims cast themselves down to kiss the ground and pray, and many were overcome

A fifteenth-century woodcut of a view of Venice. Ships left regularly from here to take pilgrims from all over Europe to Jerusalem and the Holy Land.

with emotion: some wandered around beating their chests; some sat down and sobbed violently; some lay prostrate, as still as corpses; and some of the women pilgrims 'shrieked as though in labour'.

The Christians were then led off to their lodgings. As a friar, Felix was allowed to stay in the Franciscan convent on Mount Sion, in the south of the city, while the laymen went to the partially ruined Hospital of St John. Once settled in and officially welcomed by the Franciscans, the pilgrims began their hectic round of sightseeing. There was no shortage of holy places – almost every prominent rock, gnarled old olive tree or mysterious ruin seems to have had some association with a biblical event. Felix mentions visiting a stone where Peter stood after denying Jesus for the third time; the corner of a house where the Virgin Mary waited while Jesus was being tried; the house where James, patron saint of Compostela, was beheaded by Herod Agrippa; the stone that marked where the resurrected Christ greeted the three Mary's – and so on.

The climax to the sightseeing came on 14 July with a visit to the Church of the Holy Sepulchre. After the Saracen wardens had let them in, the pilgrims formally processed around the church, paying devotions at the numerous holy places. All the while they held candles – Felix noted with disapproval that some pilgrims felt superior for having candles 'curiously twisted and decorated with gilding and painting' – and sang hymns, kissed relics and collected indulgences. The procession ended at the site of the tomb of Jesus, after which the pilgrims sat in various corners of the church and

ate a meal. After the celebration of midnight Mass – at which over-zealous priests competed in an unseemly fashion to conduct the service at the high altar – the Saracens entered the church to eject the Christians and chased them like foxes in a hen coop, running about with 'frightful yells'.

So ended the first visit to the Church of the Holy Sepulchre. The pilgrims would return two more times. On the third occasion – the night before most of the pilgrims were departing for home – Felix recorded that the atmosphere was spoiled by a plague of fleas, a group of Syrian Christians who were banging pieces of metal as part of their ritual and the fact that rather than worship and pray, many pilgrims slept, ate, gossiped and even – contrary to Father Paul's strict instructions – scratched their names on the holy stonework.

Apart from the sights in Jerusalem, there was plenty to see outside the city. One of the highlights was Bethlehem. Braving a group of Bedouins who roughly manhandled them outside the town – one of them charged Felix with a lance and speared his hat – the pilgrims proceeded to the recently refurbished Church of the Holy Nativity. Beneath the choir stood a white marble manger on a marble pavement, and Felix registered his unease at the disparity between the sumptuousness of the shrine and what must have been the humble simplicity of the original stable. The pilgrims were also shown the cave where the bodies of the children slain by Herod the Great had been thrown, and one or two of the pilgrims had a quick look for a relic to take back home.

Another highlight was a two-day excursion to the River Jordan. Some pilgrims plunged in fully dressed to endow their clothing with good fortune; some draped wool and linen in the river, with a view to making garments from the blessed material; others filled bottles and flasks or dipped small bells into the water. Felix kept cool by sitting on the river bed, the water up to his neck, drinking in the scene.

Officially the pilgrimage ended on 22 July, although a few people, including Felix, stayed on to visit Sinai and Egypt. In 1483 Felix returned home from Alexandria, but

ABOVE: The Church of the Holy Sepulchre, the most holy pilgrimage shrine in Jerusalem, marks the site of Christ's burial and resurrection.

it is possible to get an idea of the itinerary from Jerusalem to Venice from his account of his homeward voyage in 1480. That journey turned out to be a nightmare. The ship carrying the pilgrims, most of whom were exhausted from their whirlwind tour and suffering from sickness, sailed from Jaffa to Cyprus, then made for Rhodes and Crete. Food consisted of tainted meat, stale bread and worm-riddled biscuit, while water ran seriously short, with the pilgrims forced to buy discoloured water from the crew for more than the price of wine. The sheep, goats, mules and pigs on board were deprived of water rations and pathetically licked the deck for any moisture. At Rhodes the pilgrims witnessed the ghoulish aftermath of a failed Turkish siege; corpses littered the seashore, and the city walls and towers were reduced to rubble. The cheap prices and delicious Malvoisie wine of Crete provided some respite, but then came a terrifying storm, with lightning, fierce winds and mountainous waves. While most of the pilgrims prayed aloud, and some vowed to go on pilgrimage to Rome or Compostela if only they might escape, Felix himself could not help but think of the words of the ancient sage Anacharsis 'who said that those who are at sea cannot be counted among either the living or the dead . . . they were only removed from death by the space of four fingers, four fingers being the thickness of the sides of a ship. Also, when asked which ships were the safest, he replied: "Those which lie on dry ground, and not in the sea."' No doubt Felix also prayed to God and the saints; but his response to the crisis – even if skewed towards the entertainment of the Ulm friars – again indicates a mind in tune with the humanism of his day, with its delight in classical erudition.

The voyagers survived the storm and made their way up the Adriatic, past Ragusa (Dubrovnik) to Parenzo and from there to Venice. Felix must have voiced the feelings of all medieval travellers to the Holy Land, and possibly of pilgrims everywhere, when he declared at the end of his account of his first voyage to Palestine: 'It requires courage and audacity to attempt this pilgrimage. That many are prompted to it by sinful rashness and idle curiosity cannot be doubted; but to reach the holy places and to return to one's home active and well is the especial gift of God.' Felix certainly had curiosity, but it was underpinned by a deep religious sensibility. When, in later times, this latter quality came to be eroded by scepticism and scientific reason, the 'pilgrim' became curious about places and objects simply for the sake of interest or for self-improvement. He became in effect a tourist.

CHANGING ATTITUDES

The late Middle Ages – roughly from the mid-fourteenth century to the start of the sixteenth – saw profound changes in European society that affected the lives and attitudes of all classes, influencing their perspective on religion, the Church and religious observances such as pilgrimage. Perhaps the single most dramatic agent of change was the Black Death, which from 1347 to 1351 claimed the lives of about twenty million people throughout the continent, approximately one third of the total population. The plague had a knock-on effect, creating tensions in the fabric of society: in devastated villages and hamlets, surviving peasant workers suddenly found they were in great demand and could exert leverage for better pay and working conditions. The denial of these by government authorities led to increased social tension and in some places violent civil unrest. In 1358 French peasants, suffering from the effects of the Black Death, the war with England and other grievances, rose up against their feudal masters; and in England in 1381, a peasant army converged on London demanding radical social and economic reforms. Both revolts were crushed, but the underlying problems and pressure for change remained.

Meanwhile, the prestige of the Church was steadily diminishing. In 1303 King Philip IV of France responded to aggressive assertions of papal authority by Pope Boniface VIII by sending in troops to capture him. Although they failed, the fact that they had dared to assault Christendom's most revered figure dimmed the aura of papal supremacy. Then in 1309, the French pope Clement V, under pressure from his monarch, moved the papal residence from Rome to Avignon and into what was called the 'Babylonian Exile'. Although the papacy eventually returned to the Eternal City in 1377, the following year marked the start of the Great Schism – the election of two rival popes, one at Rome, the other back at Avignon, each supported by regional factions. An attempt in 1409 by a general Church council to restore the status of the papacy by deposing the two popes and electing a third ended with the farcical situation of three popes claiming to be the true pontiff. The predicament was finally

'The Flagellants of Doornick', a coloured miniature painted in 1349. As plague swept across Europe, this extreme ascetic form of penance arose in spite of the Church's disapproval and attempts to suppress it.

resolved at the Council of Constance (1414–18) and the election of Martin V as sole pope. But the protracted and unedifying feuding, compromise and corruption had left their mark.

One of those who voiced his outrage against the Church and the papacy publicly was the radical English theologian John Wycliffe, who believed that the word of God as manifested in the Bible was the only true authority for Christians. Wycliffe attacked clerical wealth and property ownership and also, more heretically, denied the doctrine of transubstantiation – which contends that the substance of bread and wine changes into the substance of the body and blood of Christ when consecrated in the Mass. He saw the Host as nothing more than 'an effectual sign'. Wycliffe's followers, known as Lollards, continued to promulgate his ideas after his death, even producing an English translation of the Bible in the 1390s, for they believed that the Bible should be read by everyone and not remain a preserve of the priesthood. But in 1401 Henry IV introduced severe measures to stamp out Lollardy, and some years later the movement lost further momentum after a failed uprising led by the Lollard leader Sir John Oldcastle in 1414.

With their condemnation of Church practices and hierarchy and their deep suspicion of enjoyment, the Lollards were, not surprisingly, critical of pilgrimage. This is shown in a contemporary account by a Lollard priest named William Thorpe, who described his interrogation for heresy by Thomas Arundel, Archbishop of Canterbury, in 1407. When asked who he thought a 'true pilgrim' was, Thorpe said it was someone who travels 'towards the bliss of heaven' by eschewing evil and embracing the Christian virtues and obeying God's commandments. By contrast, Thorpe excoriated those pilgrims who were ignorant of their faith but nevertheless set off on journeys 'more for the health of their bodies than of their souls! More to have richesse and prosperity of this world, than for to be enriched with virtues in their souls'. These so-called pilgrims, he continued, spent their money in dubious foreign hostelries when they could be spending it at home, helping the poor.

In fact Thorpe's view that true pilgrimage depended on personal virtue and inner godliness – and not just tramping off to some shrine – had been reiterated from the time of the Church Fathers. In the fourth century, St John Chrysostom, for instance, had said there was no necessity to make long journeys and that people should pray to

God at home. St Jerome, who had done so much to encourage pilgrimage, wrote that God could not be tied to one particular place on earth and that the 'court of heaven lies open to Britain and Jerusalem alike'. Closer to Thorpe's time, the fourteenth-century poet William Langland emphasized in his poem *Piers Plowman* that pilgrims to Rome or Compostela were not necessarily seeking truth: the road to truth involved the practice of Christian virtues.

So marked was the Lollard antagonism to pilgrimage that to go on one or to swear to their validity was taken as evidence of non-involvement in the heretical movement. A Lollard named William Dynet, for example, renounced the error of his ways by swearing he would support the cult of saints and would 'nevermore despyse pylgremage'. Yet going on pilgrimage did not save the English visionary Margery Kempe from charges of Lollardy and threats of burning. Born in about 1373 in Lynn, Norfolk, Margery married her husband John Kempe in 1393 and proceeded to have fourteen children by him. When she was about forty she took a vow of chastity and began to go on pilgrimages to Canterbury, Jerusalem, Rome, Santiago de Compostela and other smaller shrines (she is often compared to Chaucer's Wife of Bath, a cheerful worldly soul, five-times married, who had also been to Christendom's major shrines). But Margery was anything but worldly: her continual visions of Jesus and the saints, and her propensity for 'great weeping and boisterous sobbing' in public places, attracted constant bewilderment, scorn and rejection. In Venice, for example, to where she had travelled with a company of fellow pilgrims, 'her countrymen forsook her and went away from her, leaving her alone. And some of them said that they would not go with her for a hundred pound.' Apart from her uninhibited display of emotions, Margery also provoked hostility by her outspoken criticism of the clergy. Nevertheless, although sometimes hampered by the Church authorities, she was still able to carry out her spiritual journeys and, along with insults and threats, she received much goodwill, charity and fellowship along the way, as her autobiographical *Book of Margery Kempe* describes.

If in later medieval times pilgrimages were losing some of their spiritual rigour, as the criticisms of the Lollards and the tales of Chaucer imply, they were only following a general social trend in which, for example, the increase of commerce and the growth of universities reflected and stimulated a heightened interest in the external world and knowledge for its own sake, not necessarily for the sake of God. This curiosity in the world, traditionally seen as a characteristic of the Renaissance, can be discerned in some late medieval pilgrim guidebooks and pilgrims' accounts, which delight in details of foreign dress, customs and language in a way that seems inconceivable in pilgrim itineraries of the first millennium. Felix Fabri (see pages 115–121), for example, often cannot resist describing details of his surroundings simply out of sheer fascination, such as the 'wondrous fishes' he saw in the port of Jaffa – 'some were large and quite round, like a winnowing fan. Some had heads like dogs, with long ears hanging down'. He reports on terebinth trees in a way that would do a botanist proud: '[Terebinths] are fine trees, which grow chiefly in Syria, and from which a gum sweats forth . . . they are twofold, that is to say, male and female, and bear a twofold fruit. The male bears a reddish fruit of the size of a small lentil.'

One of the strangest late medieval pilgrim accounts was the *Travels of Sir John Mandeville*, which, historian Jonathan Sumption has noted, 'was the first really popular book to portray travel as an adventure and a romance'. First published in 1357 in French, the *Travels* were purportedly written by an English knight of

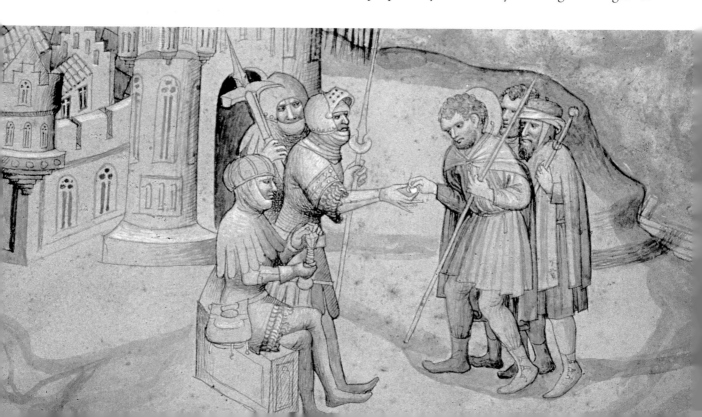

St Albans who set off on pilgrimage to the Holy Land in 1322 and then made his way to the lands of the East, which he describes with a keen eye for the exotic. In fact most scholars believe that the book is mainly a compilation of accounts by other travellers and that the author was possibly a citizen of Liège named Jean d'Outremeuse. Among the scenes the author describes are the Pyramids of Egypt, which he calls the 'granaries of Joseph', dismissing the idea that they are 'sepulchres of great lords'. At the Dead Sea he tells of apple trees whose fruit contains coal and cinders; in Ethiopia there are people who have only one leg with one large foot with which they shade themselves when lying down; and in India 'men worship the ox' and 'women shave their beards, and the men not'. He also tells of the realms of the powerful emperor of China; of Prester John, a mysterious Christian ruler of Ethiopia; and of the terrestrial Paradise – though he admits he has never been there himself.

In a world in which the momentum for exploration and discovery was gathering pace, the *Travels*, filled with facts, fables and legends, became one of the most popular books of the Middle Ages, and was translated into English, Latin, German and various other languages. The author himself seemed to sum up the spirit of the times when he referred to the fact that in his day 'many men have great liking to hear speak of strange things of diverse countries'. It was this 'curiosity' that informed the spirit of the dawning Renaissance and also, for many, undermined the devotional journey. St Augustine had railed against the effects of *curiositas* in his *Confessions*, stating that people gaze in wonder at mountains, huge waves, wide rivers, the great ocean or the stars in the sky but 'pay no attention to themselves . . . For when our hearts become repositories piled high with such worthless stock as this, it is the cause of interruption and distraction from our prayers.' It was a sentiment that found a powerful contemporary voice in the late medieval mystic Thomas à Kempis, who wrote that people who visited pilgrimage places were 'often moved by curiosity and the urge for sight-seeing, and one seldom hears that any amendment of life results, especially as their conversation is trivial and lacks true contrition.'

An early fifteenth-century illustration from the *Travels of Sir John Mandeville* showing the pilgrims approaching the gates of Jerusalem.

MODERN WAYS

FROM REFORMATION TO ROMANTICISM

In about 1512 and 1514 the Renaissance scholar and satirist Erasmus made pilgrimages to Walsingham and Canterbury, the two pre-eminent English shrines, and later drew on his experiences when he lampooned aspects of pilgrimage in his *Colloquy* entitled 'The Religious Pilgrimage'. Such was the power of his pen that some contemporaries believed his writings were partly responsible for the drop in numbers of aristocratic pilgrims travelling to the Holy Land, where the expansion of the Ottoman Turks had also made pilgrimage difficult. Certainly, when St Ignatius Loyola visited Palestine in 1523 he found few signs of pilgrim activity. Although there had been dissenting voices raised against pilgrimage before the Reformation – those of the Lollards, for example – attacks by Erasmus as well as by the Protestant Reformers (that is, those such as the Lutherans and Calvinists who 'protested' against Roman Catholicism) on what they considered to be unscriptural rituals and 'superstition' now took their toll. A Spanish canon named Francisco Molina wrote in 1550 that while more pilgrims were going to Santiago de Compostela than to Rome, 'since the damned doctrines of Luther arose, the number of pilgrims has fallen off, and especially from Germany and the wealthy from England'.

The Reformation was not, of course, a pre-planned unified movement masterminded by the German monk Martin Luther. His initial intention had been to correct abuses within the Church, not break away from it. In the end, despite efforts to effect a reconciliation, disagreements between Luther's followers and the Church, especially on issues such as clerical marriage and the authority of the Pope, proved decisive. Erasmus himself, while critical of the Church, still retained his traditional piety; and his innately peace-loving, scholarly personality shied away from the radicals and militants among the Reformers. In the end he became *persona non grata* to both the Protestants and Catholics. 'The Religious Pilgrimage', therefore, is the more interesting for being the product of an independent mind. It takes the form of a dialogue between the sceptical Menedemus and his friend Ogygius, a devout,

PREVIOUS: Crowds gather at the grotto of St Bernadette in Lourdes, France. Although established for less than 150 years, Lourdes is today the most visited pilgrimage shrine in all Christendom.

somewhat naive, believer, who has been on pilgrimage to Compostela, Walsingham and Canterbury. When asked how he found 'the good man of St James', Ogygius replies that the saint has had fewer visits than before because of the 'new opinion' that has spread throughout the world: instead of glittering with gold and jewels St James has been reduced to the 'very block that he is made of', with barely a tallow candle to boast about. Menedemus surmises that if this is true then the rest of the saints must be in jeopardy too.

Ogygius next describes his visit to Walsingham, 'the holiest name' in England, where, in a chapel 'full of marvels', a verger showed him and his companions the giant-sized middle joint of a man's finger claimed to be from the hand of St Peter. The most precious relic, however, was a phial of milk from the Virgin Mary; when Ogygius dared to ask the verger for evidence of the milk's authenticity the man looked at them 'with astonished eyes and a sort of horror' and would have ejected them all as heretics but for a tip. At Canterbury Ogygius and a companion, identifiable as Erasmus's friend John Colet, Dean of St Paul's, were shown 'a world of bones . . . skulls, chins, teeth, hands, fingers, whole arms, all of which we kissed'. Having gazed at a stockpile of precious ornaments and jewels, Colet told their guide that it would be better to use some of the riches to help the poor: the man began to 'frown and to pout out his lips, and to look upon us as he would have

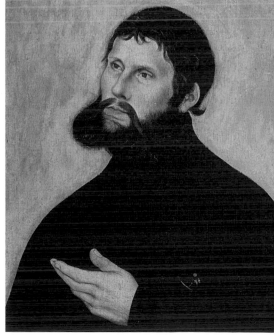

ABOVE RIGHT: Erasmus was highly critical of aspects of the Church, including pilgrimage; RIGHT: Martin Luther thought that pilgrimages were opportunities for breaking God's laws.

eaten us up'. This concern for the poor is echoed by Menedemus – representing the voice of Erasmus himself – who says that although there should be some vestments and vessels to dignify a church, the profusion of golden tombs, candlesticks and images were an extravagance when 'our brothers and sisters . . . are ready to die from hunger and thirst'.

The social argument against the Church's wealth, pomp and pride – and by association against such activities as processions and pilgrimages – had surfaced throughout the history of Christianity; and now it found powerful new expression through Luther and the Protestant Reformers. Born in Saxony in 1483 to humble parents, Luther became an Augustinian monk and, later, a professor of theology at the University of Wittenberg, newly established by Frederick, Elector of Saxony. In 1515 he started working on a series of lectures on St Paul's Letter to the Romans, a text that convinced him that people could not save themselves by doing good works (including going on pilgrimage) but only by receiving the grace of God – by being 'justified' by their faith. At the same time Luther was increasingly concerned about the lax behaviour of the clergy, their lack of spirituality and their concern for their own temporal advancement. Matters came to a head over the sale of indulgences. When a Dominican friar named Johan Tetzel began selling indulgences near Wittenberg to raise money for the debt-ridden Archbishop Albert of Magdeburg and for Pope Leo X's building programme, Luther reacted by nailing his famous Ninety-Five Theses, attacking indulgences and inviting debate about them, to the door of the church at Wittenberg Castle. Cutting to the heart of the Church's teaching on relics and purgatory, and undermining its authority, such an aggressive public challenge could not go unanswered. In 1521 Luther was excommunicated and declared an outlaw by the Church; but he was given personal protection by Frederick, Elector of Saxony, who disregarded the fact that Luther could not have approved of his own enormous collection of relics. Helped by the relatively new technology of printing, the views of Luther and his followers spread across Europe. At the heart of their 'new opinion' lay the primacy of the Bible, the Word of God, as opposed to the authority of the Church through the pope or its councils.

In Germany itself, the local princes, motivated more by considerations of power than theology, divided into pro-Protestant and pro-Catholic factions, whose mutual enmity was for a time resolved by the 1555 Peace of Augsburg, which laid down that a ruler's faith should determine that of his people. Elsewhere, Protestant ideas were developed more systematically: by Huldreich Zwingli in Zurich and, especially, by John Calvin in Geneva. In England, Henry VIII broke with Rome over the issue of divorcing his childless wife Catherine of Aragon. In 1534 Henry declared himself head of the Church of England and in 1536 set about suppressing monasteries and appropriating their lands for himself and his favourites. Henry himself showed no great enthusiasm for doctrinal change; but the ideas of the Reformers gained ground during the reign of his successor, Edward VI, and, after the reactionary years of Mary Tudor (1553–8), during the time of Elizabeth I.

The Reformers damaged pilgrimage both by attacking its underlying theological assumptions and by physically destroying shrines and relics. Luther, for example, in his *Address to the Christian Nobility of the German Nation* (1521) stated that going on pilgrimage deluded people into believing they were performing important virtuous acts. God, he said, had commanded us to look after our families and neighbours – not to go off to Rome on a spending spree, masking curiosity or 'devilish delusion' with piety. Pilgrimages, he continued, were occasions for sinning, for flouting God's commandments, for attracting ne'er-do-wells such as beggars and vagabonds. Secular and religious authorities should persuade would-be pilgrims to spend the money and time they were reserving for the journey on their families and the poor.

The Reformers also attacked relics, purgatory and prayers to the dead; and with their emphasis on justification by faith, and a direct relationship with God unmediated by saintly intercessors, they challenged the traditional idea of the 'communion of saints' – the great family of Christians whose members, on earth and in the afterlife, are locked in a reciprocal spiritual relationship. Removing the idea that a penitential journey to a shrine could help a relative in purgatory, or that a saint could intervene in human affairs, undercut the theological basis for pilgrimage. Pious motives for going to Rome or Jerusalem may have cloaked worldly desires for a taste of freedom, travel and new experiences – but the devotional aspect gave the journey an all-important focus, even if there were tempting distractions. Without a religious goal there was nothing to stop pilgrimage becoming a sightseeing trip, in which the novelties of travel become an end in themselves.

In countries where the ideas of the Reformers now held sway, people did not suddenly reject the old piety en masse. But the pressure to change was powerful. In England the clergy were instructed to preach against pilgrimage to relics, and between 1536 and 1540 hundreds of monasteries and shrines were dissolved up and down the land. Bells were melted down, wooden choir stalls torn out and lead stripped from the roofs. A contemporary chronicler remarked that 'all the notable images unto the which were made any special pilgrimages and offerings, were utterly taken away'. Relics were declared to be fakes and broken up or burnt. To take a typical example, the Bishop of Rochester declared the most sacred relic of Hayles Abbey – a phial said to contain the Holy Blood of Christ – to be nothing but 'honey clarified and coloured with saffron' and destroyed it. It was not only the relics that were stripped away: in Elizabethan times the Royal Injunctions of 1559 decreed that commissioners should 'destroy all shrines, coverings of shrines, all tables, candlesticks, trindals and rolls of wax, pictures, paintings, and all monuments of feigned miracles, pilgrimages, idolatry, and superstition, so that there remain no memory of the same in walls, glass windows, or elsewhere within their churches and houses.' It was hard, nonetheless, to wipe out the memories. At Walsingham a government official alleged that there was a woman who had dreamed up 'a false tale' of a miracle effected by the 'Image', i.e. statue, of Our Lady after it had been carried off from the shrine and burned at Chelsea. Her punishment for declaring this story was to be confined to the stocks then paraded around the market place in a cart as a 'reporter of false tales'. The official added his view that 'the said Image is not yet out of some of their heads'.

But if the impulse to go on pilgrimage in search of miracles and cures is age-old and universal, what happened to it in the Protestant lands? Without the healing power of saints to sustain them, many would have turned to local herbalists, 'wise women' and white witches for medicinal help. It may also be significant, as historian Ronald Finucane has observed, that spa resorts became more popular during Reformation times, with cured invalids leaving their crutches behind as they had formerly done at

The remains of Rievaulx Abbey, Yorkshire. A vast and wealthy medieval Cistercian monastery, it rapidly fell into ruin after Henry VIII's men destroyed its roof and confiscated its treasures in the 1530s.

pilgrimage shrines. Another altogether different approach to pilgrimage was suggested by Erasmus in 'The Religious Pilgrimage'. When Menedemus mentions doing the 'Roman Stations', which traditionally meant visiting certain churches and altars in Rome, he goes on to explain exactly what his are: 'I walk about my house; I go to my study, and take care of my daughter's chastity; thence I go into my shop, and see what my servants are doing; then into the kitchen, and see if anything be amiss there; and so from one place to another, to observe what my wife and what my children are doing, taking care that every one be at his business. These are my Roman Stations.' In this view, pilgrimage is a way of life based around a domestic circuit of personal responsibility rather than a linear journey to an external destination.

Erasmus's idea of a bourgeois *peregrinatio* signified a radical departure from the traditional notion of pilgrimage. Towards the end of the sixteenth century a more secular approach to pilgrimage travel was witnessed by guidebooks such as the Protestant Jerome Turler's *De Peregrinatione*. This work addressed the practicalities of travel abroad in a way familiar from past pilgrim guides but, despite its title, it was concerned primarily with the importance of discovering and learning from strange but potentially useful foreign customs. This was pilgrimage as a fact-finding tour. During this period there were also pilgrim handbooks that did not presuppose any physical journey at all. In Luis de Granada's popular *Le Vray Chemin* ('The True Way'), for example, pilgrimage is imagined rather than actually undergone, which for Luis had the advantage of avoiding the pitfalls of physical travel with all its seductive curiosities. A similar idea of mental or imagined pilgrimage is also found in the *Spiritual Exercises* of St Ignatius Loyola, published in 1548, which sets out a meditative journey that calls upon the reader to conjure up certain events and scenes from the Gospels, and to use them as tools to help overcome his or her sense of sin. In a similar vein, in 1500, the Strasbourg preacher Johann Geiler declared that he had worked out exactly how long it would take to walk to the churches of Rome and back, so that a prisoner unable to go there could re-enact the journey in his mind by pacing round his cell for the right amount of time (forty-two days).

The principle of being able to make a pilgrimage through the mind and heart also lay behind the Stations of the Cross. These fourteen representations of the Passion of Christ are linked to specific points on the Via Dolorosa in Jerusalem, the route traditionally taken by Jesus from his condemnation by Pilate to the site of his crucifixion and burial. Each image alludes to a scene from the Passion and is used as a focus for specific devotions. From the fifteenth and sixteenth centuries it became increasingly common for images of the stations to be set up in churches all over Europe – these visual signs enabling the faithful who could not make the physical journey to Jerusalem to be 'transported' there through an imagined empathetic journey. In some cases, to make the pilgrimage seem especially authentic, the stations were spaced so that they replicated the exact distance between the original ones in Jerusalem.

THE AGE OF REASON

During the first half of the seventeenth century Europe was disfigured by widespread war, waged in the name of religion but fuelled in the main by national politics. The Thirty Years War (1618–48) pitted the Catholic Habsburg Holy Roman Empire and Spain against the Protestant German princes and their allies, including, at different times, Holland, Denmark, Sweden, England and even Catholic France, anxious to curb Habsburg power. The war continued until 1648 when the Peace of Westphalia realigned territorial boundaries and confirmed the principle that a state's religion should be determined by its ruler. In England, the religious tensions created among Anglicans, Puritans (Anglicans who wanted to see the Church of England further 'purified' of Catholic elements of worship), Catholics and Dissenters (non-Anglican Protestant groups such as the Independents, Presbyterians and Baptists) were a constant problem to the Stuart kings. But the victory of Oliver Cromwell and the Parliamentarian forces during the Civil War – sometimes called the 'Puritan Revolution' – and the establishment of the Commonwealth (1649–60) led to the ascendancy of the Puritans' interpretation of 'true godliness'. This included an emphasis on high personal moral standards, education, plain dress and reverence for Sunday.

The Puritans also stressed the primacy of the Word of God, at the expense of ceremony. To them the idea of going on pilgrimage, with its presupposition of relics and a cult of saints, was an alien one. Yet the pilgrimage of one Puritan, John Bunyan, has become one of the most famous in the world. Bunyan's *The Pilgrim's Progress*, first published in 1678 and expanded in 1684, is an allegorical pilgrimage of the soul related in such fresh, vivid, down-to-earth language that it quickly became universally popular, even among the barely literate. In a tradition of allegorical narrative that went back to Guillaume de Deguileville's *Pilgrimage of the Life of Man* (*c*. 1330), Bunyan's story revolves around a pilgrim named Christian who leaves his home in the City of Destruction to journey to the Celestial City. Along the way he encounters various trials, tribulations and temptations, but also encouragement from characters such as Piety and Charity. Eventually he crosses the River of Death and arrives at the Celestial City, which 'shone like the sun, the streets also were paved with gold, and in them walked many men with crowns on their heads, palms in their hands, and golden harps to sing praises withal'. To create his masterpiece, Bunyan drew on his own conflict with the Royalist authorities of the Restoration – he was imprisoned for his faith off and on between 1660 and 1672 – as well as his personal spiritual crises and his knowledge of the Bible and popular preaching. Bunyan's pilgrimage is not a physical journey, nor does it resemble the concentrated meditations of Ignatius Loyola or the domestic prudence of Erasmus's 'Roman Stations': it is a luminous journey of the soul, imagined but rooted in the Word of God – a spiritual trek from the human condition of sin to the God-given state of grace.

Religious pilgrimage in the Protestant lands of post-Reformation Europe may have fallen out of fashion, lingering on as a source of metaphors for Christian thinkers, but the urge to go on journeys did not go away. In the eighteenth century, the so-called Age of Reason or Enlightenment, when the value of reason and empirical science prevailed among Europe's intelligentsia, young men and sometimes women set out to broaden their minds, widen their knowledge and improve their aesthetic taste in cities such as Paris, Geneva, Cologne, Florence, Rome, Venice and Naples. Their 'shrines' tended to be splendid works of architecture or art collections; their 'pilgrim badges' were often antiquities, brought back home to adorn elegant drawing rooms and libraries.

The Grand Tour, as it became known, had many similarities to pilgrimage journeys: like medieval pilgrims, eighteenth-century gentlemen were swindled by ferrymen,

The *Plan of the Road from the City of Destruction to the Celestial City* – a nineteenth-century engraving for John Bunyan's *The Pilgrim's Progress*.

bitten by fleas and fleeced by innkeepers, and they too had to traverse the treacherous Alps with guides, pay tolls and bribe officials. They would also have shared the same excitement – or disappointment – at reaching their long-imagined goals. But whereas the pilgrim, at least notionally, was seeking the realm of the Divine and the miraculous, the tourist primarily sought new experiences, knowledge and pleasure. The Grand Tour became particularly popular with young Englishmen after peace descended on Europe with the end of the Seven Years War in 1763. Many, used to the restrained piety of the Church of England, found the unfamiliar sights and sounds of continental Catholicism noteworthy: the shrines with gaily painted images of saints, the constant sound of bells, the religious processions, the high profile of monks and priests. But these manifestations of religion were more of a curiosity than a stimulus to awe. An Irish traveller named Catherine Wilmot did find Milan Cathedral magnificent, but the local friar who talked to her of relics and miracles she dismissed as a 'wholesale camel-swallower'. James Boswell, Dr Johnson's biographer, also admired the cathedral – but for its 'many good pictures'. Rome itself was often disappointing, with its beggars, narrow, dirty streets and general air of poverty. Yet compensations were to be found in the noble ruins, squares, fountains, columns and countless statues and paintings. The catacombs were visited, as were the main churches – Boswell even enjoyed a service at St Peter's. The tourists studied their guidebooks, sketched, painted, scribbled down their impressions, bought their souvenirs: these were their devotions. Eventually, the French Revolution and the Napoleonic Wars severely limited travel on the continent. There was a surge of activity after the wars (which ended in 1815) – as Samuel Taylor Coleridge put it: 'Tour, Journey, Voyage, Lounge, Ride, Walk,/Skim, Sketch, Excursion, Travel-talk – /For move you must! 'Tis now the rage,/The law and fashion of the Age.' But from then on the Grand Tour never really recovered its former prestige.

In Britain, during these bellicose times, would-be travellers were forced to find substitutes: Snowdonia for the Alps, or Cumbria for the Italian lakes. One celebrated home-grown site was Tintern Abbey, whose ruins beside the River Wye in Wales inspired J. M. W. Turner and William Wordsworth. The abbey's ivy-clad stone shell was nigh-on perfect for the Romantic sensibility – which delighted in nature in its wildest forms – though Revd William Gilpin, author of a best-selling handbook on

the Tintern area, thought the gable ends too regular: 'a mallet judiciously used,' he suggested, '(but who durst use it?) might be of service in fracturing some of them.' With no relics, altars, statues or chapels to lure the pilgrims to Tintern, visitors had to fall back on their imaginations to recreate a sense of the numinous, aided by the surrounding tree-clad hills and swiftly flowing river. Although there were no bells, candles or incense to regale the senses, the spirits could be lifted by a Welsh harper hired at nearby Chepstow or by a midnight picnic, lit by flaming torches. With no officially sanctioned religious pilgrimages to turn to, British Romantics of the late eighteenth and early nineteenth centuries had to invent their own.

ABOVE: The nineteenth-century artist George Frederic Watts gave the ruins Tintern Abbey a suitably spiritual aspect in this painting.

LOURDES

The great age of medieval pilgrimage ended with the Reformation. In Protestant countries shrines were dismantled and the spiritual structure that validated them, such as the belief in the power of saints and relics, was largely destroyed. There were exceptions: Holywell in Wales, for example, has attracted pilgrims from medieval times to the present day without interruption. And there were probably many more unrecorded local shrines that continued to draw small numbers of pilgrims. In Catholic countries pilgrimage was still a meritorious act. But there, too, blew the cold winds of scepticism, reason and secularization. Of the great medieval shrines, Santiago de Compostela retained its pilgrimage tradition the best and even experienced a revival in the late seventeenth century before declining in the eighteenth, with the onset of the turmoil caused by the French Revolution and the Napoleonic Wars.

In the nineteenth and early twentieth centuries, pilgrimage was reawakened: new pilgrimages came into being, old ones were resuscitated. The reasons are difficult to establish. There may have been a reaction to the increasing industrialization and mechanization of society, resulting in a longing for rituals that gave a sense of *communitas*. And at a time when science, in particular the theory of evolution, was challenging the authority of the Bible and old certainties of faith, pilgrimage may have partially answered a need for direct religious experience – a thirst for connecting with places and people seemingly in close contact with the divine.

One of the significant characteristics of the new pilgrimages was that they revolved around not the holy relics or images typical of medieval times but reputed miraculous apparitions, especially of the Virgin Mary. France in particular proved receptive to these apparitions (sociologists of religion are tempted to connect them with the fact that the country was recovering from one of the most turbulent periods of its history, with first the Revolution and then the Napoleonic Wars). Between July 1830 and September 1831 a French novice named Catherine Labouré saw, in her convent chapel in Paris, four apparitions of the Virgin Mary, who commanded her to have a medal struck bearing the Virgin's image (in the following years millions of 'Miraculous Medals' were duly made). In 1846 two children at La Salette near Grenoble saw a vision of the Virgin, who appeared as a radiant form wearing a gold-sequinned robe and silver shoes. Then on 11 February 1858, a poor, illiterate fourteen-year-old girl named Bernadette Soubirous witnessed an apparition of the Virgin in a grotto of a riverside cliff near her home town Lourdes. This and subsequent apparitions transformed an obscure French Pyrenean town into the most frequented place of Christian pilgrimage in the world.

The apparition was the first of eighteen that Bernadette was to receive over the following five months. At first, it was not certain who or what the young woman of the apparition was. Bernadette simply referred to her as Aqueró, local dialect for 'that one'. The reactions of local people were mixed. One of the nuns who taught Bernadette accused her of playing pranks. Others believed she had seen the ghost of a devout Lourdes woman named Elisa Latapie, who had died the previous autumn. After the sixth apparition the civic authorities began to get involved, the local police commissioner trying in vain to pressurize Bernadette into admitting her story was a hoax. After the ninth apparition, when Bernadette was seen to scrabble around in the mud inside the grotto and uncover a spring of water, she was interrogated by a local magistrate, who made her promise not to return to the spot. But the pull of the cave proved irresistible.

The parish priest, Father Peyramale, was also unsympathetic at first. But he was forced to confront the issue head on when, after the thirteenth apparition, Bernadette informed him that Aqueró had instructed her to tell 'the priests' that people were to come to the grotto in procession and that a chapel must be built. Peyramale retorted testily that he would have to know the apparition's identity before there was any question of processions or a chapel. During the sixteenth apparition, on 25 March, the feast of the Annunciation, Bernadette duly asked the young woman who she was. She replied in the local dialect: 'Que soy era Immaculada Councepciou' – 'I am the Immaculate Conception'. The answer unambiguously referred to the Catholic doctrine of the Virgin Mary being untainted by original sin from the moment of conception.

ABOVE: Bernadette Soubirous in 1860, two years after the Virgin Mary appeared to her in a remote mountain grotto in the Pyrenees.

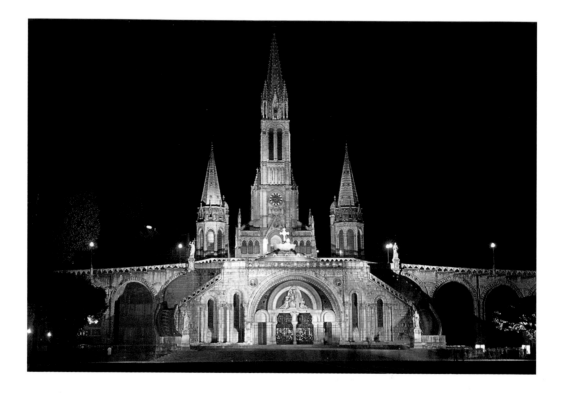

It seemed incredible to Peyramale that an uneducated peasant girl could have made up such a phrase, and from then on he became one of Bernadette's staunchest supporters.

There were still two apparitions to come. On 7 April, in the presence of about 1,000 onlookers, Bernadette appeared to let the flame of the candle she was holding lick her hand without showing signs of pain – an event that afterwards many hailed as a miracle. The final apparition occurred on 16 July, after the grotto had been cordoned off by the authorities to keep the crowds away, and Bernadette was forced to catch her final glimpse of Aqueró from the far side of the river.

For Bernadette the apparitions were the climax of her time on earth. There were no more visions, voices or beatific states. The remaining years of her short life were

ABOVE: The Basilica of the Rosary in Lourdes was completed in 1899 to accommodate the ever-growing numbers of pilgrims to the shrine. Above it rise the spires of the Basilica of the Immaculate Conception.

relatively uneventful and coloured by her constant struggle against illness, a sad irony since Lourdes would become known as a healing shrine. In 1860 she left her poverty-stricken family to live in the local hospice run by the Sisters of Charity. Six years later she was admitted to the Sisters' mother house at Nevers in central France. There she resided for the rest of her life, removed from the world, consoled by the memory of that radiant, smiling young woman. She died in 1879 at the age of thirty-five.

While Bernadette gradually faded into obscurity after the apparitions, Lourdes and its grotto grew steadily more famous. One reason for this was a series of seemingly miraculous healings at the shrine. Other important factors were the perceived encouragement from the imperial household of Louis Napoleon III and his wife, Empress Eugénie, as well as the energetic support of the dynamic Catholic thinker and journalist Louis Veuillot. But although popular enthusiasm for Lourdes began to grow, the Church treated the affair with caution – not wishing to invite charges of credulity from its critics – and investigated Bernadette's apparitions through a commission, which after four years of deliberating declared them genuine in 1862. The Church also began to build the chapel Aqueró had requested on land it had bought above the grotto. In 1866 the crypt of the sanctuary was completed (the basilica itself was finished five years later); and in the same year the railway came to Lourdes, greatly increasing the influx of pilgrims from all over France. One major motive for making the pilgrimage – as it still is – was the hope of a cure for sickness. The first recognized healings at Lourdes occurred as early as March 1858, during the time of Bernadette's apparitions. Again, the Church trod carefully with these and other alleged cures and set up a commission to investigate them. Later on, in 1883, the Medical Bureau was founded to bring more rigour and impartiality to the process of recognizing cures (and the Medical Bureau was supplemented by another medical committee in 1947). It is a measure of the Church's caution that, of the many thousands of reported cures, fewer than a hundred have been formally recognized.

Lourdes continued to grow in prestige throughout the closing decades of the nineteenth century. In 1873, three years after France's humiliating defeat in the Franco-Prussian war, a national annual pilgrimage to Lourdes was inaugurated in the month of August by the Assumptionists, a religious order who saw the pilgrimage as a way of reasserting Christian values against a tide of secularism and, as historian

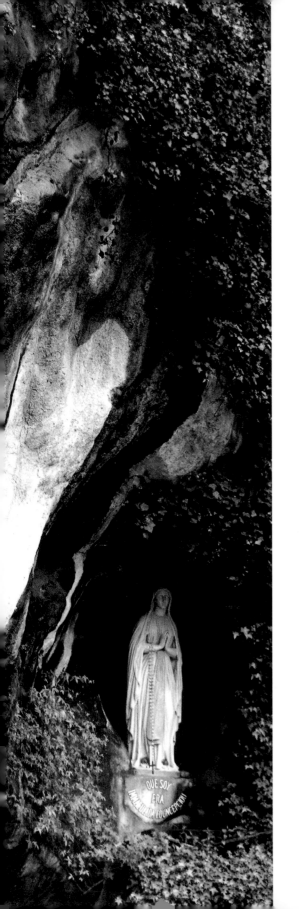

Ruth Harris has noted, 'to encapsulate and channel a mood of national soul searching'. Numbers of pilgrims increased year by year, with more than 30,000 arriving by train in August 1897, having endured cramped, stifling carriages with the sick and dying laid out on stretchers, attended by doctors, nurses, nuns, friends and relations.

On arrival at Lourdes the pilgrims were confronted, as they still are, with a town of two distinct parts, the main residential and commercial area and the Domain of Our Lady, the land around the grotto. The Domain is marked by the spire of the neo-Gothic Basilica of the Immaculate Conception, which dominates a complex of three buildings, the other two being the crypt and a chapel known as the Basilica of the Rosary, built in the Romano-Byzantine style. Unifying the complex are two long curving concrete ramps that rise from the ground on arches to the level of the main sanctuary, like the pincers of a giant crustacean. As for the grotto, it is still the town's spiritual epicentre. A broad esplanade was built beside it, allowing the pilgrim crowds to gather there to pray, light candles or proceed to the nearby baths to immerse themselves in freezing water piped from the grotto's spring.

What is curious about Lourdes is not so much that it became a Marian shrine but that it became the pre-eminent one. Certainly its setting has helped. The cliffs, river, woods and mountains combine to create a mystique that rampant commercialism has failed to dispel. Bernadette's story also carries a compelling mythic power,

A statue of the Virgin Mary today stands in the grotto at Lourdes on the exact spot where she appeared to the young Bernadette Soubirous in 1858.

especially in the way that events slowly gather momentum, drawing in more and more people until even 'hardened officials' cannot resist their force. It is also interesting that Bernadette was not the only person to see apparitions at Lourdes: a number of local children claimed similar visions soon after her experiences. Most of these were dismissed as false, but a few had an air of authenticity, especially those experienced by a girl named Marie Courrech, who was highly regarded for her innocence and strong faith. Yet only Bernadette was officially accredited as the unique recipient of apparitions of the Virgin.

Another curious aspect of the Lourdes story is the nature of Aqueró, whom Bernadette described as a girl of about her own age dressed in simple clothes, rather than the maternal figure of most other Marian apparitions. Indeed, Bernadette did not at first identify her as Mary; and in an area in which belief in folklore was deeply rooted it must have seemed significant to some that she referred to the girl as a *damizéla*, a word often used to mean a fairy. The turning point came when Aqueró declared unequivocally that she was the Immaculate Conception. For the Church, these words could mean none other than the Virgin Mary. The statement also seemed to endorse the doctrine of the Immaculate Conception, which had been formally defined by Pope Pius IX in 1854, only four years before the apparitions – a factor that has naturally aroused the suspicions of sceptics.

Yet even with the Church's endorsement of the apparitions Lourdes' success cannot be fully explained: pilgrimage sites cannot thrive on official patronage alone. The answer may lie in the fact that Lourdes has maintained its reputation as a place of physical, spiritual and emotional healing, a place that gives hope to those for whom all other remedies have failed. It may be that some physical conditions apparently cured there have had psychosomatic rather than 'organic' causes, as sceptics tend to believe (though this does not invalidate the idea of a miraculous cure); or that some cures have more to do with mental determination than supernatural agency; or that witnessing the sick and dying bearing their travails patiently, and the selflessness of their helpers, not only lifts the spirit but has a positive physical effect. In short, the causes for cures effected at Lourdes, partial or permanent, must ultimately remain a mystery; but many have no hesitation in calling that mystery God.

KNOCK

In 1879, twenty-one years after Bernadette Soubirous saw an apparition of the Virgin Mary at Lourdes, a group of about fifteen people saw another seemingly miraculous appearance of her at the village of Knock in County Mayo in the west of Ireland. Like Lourdes, Knock was a poor, obscure village, suffering from the political, social and economic hardships of the times. The harvest of 1879 had failed; widespread famine had ruined livelihoods and rendered tenants unable to pay landlords. Evictions were rife (there were some 10,000 recorded between 1874 and 1881). Many emigrated to America or England. Others took heart from the newly formed Land League, which used mass rallies and intimidation to fight back against rack-renting landlords.

Unlike at Lourdes, however, the Knock apparition happened on only one occasion (lasting for about two hours) and imparted no verbal message. Yet it was enough to turn Knock into one of the world's great Marian shrines. This did not happen overnight. For the first twenty-five years after the event Knock drew a steady stream of pilgrims, but in the first quarter of the twentieth century numbers dwindled until, in 1929, the local Archbishop of Tuam unofficially endorsed the shrine by going on pilgrimage there. From then on Knock flourished. Over the next fifty years it gained increasing recognition from Rome, which culminated in 1979 – the centenary year of the apparition – with the visit of Pope John Paul II.

The shrine grew physically, too, and the village of humble cottages became a town lined with guesthouses, hotels, restaurants and souvenir shops. The original church of St John the Baptist, where the apparition had taken place, was remodelled. Next door to it the Basilica of Our Lady – a giant new church with a capacity of 20,000 people – was dedicated in 1976; a large hostel, folk museum and the more intimate Chapel of Reconciliation were added later to the site. In 1985 the first flights from the new Knock airport set the seal on the shrine's global status. Knock has few aesthetic pretensions. The rather featureless surrounding landscape cannot distract very much from the preponderance of concrete and asphalt. But the shrine area is well designed and

Knock Shrine, County Mayo. A glass-fronted chapel, attached to the southern side of the parish church, houses statues of the figures of the apparition.

functional, and from May to October the crowds filing in to attend Mass, the hum of pilgrims reciting their rosaries and the innumerable candlelit processions create their own sense of the numinous.

The extraordinary two hours that created the Knock phenomenon occurred on the rainy evening of 21 August 1879 at about seven o'clock. The parish priest's housekeeper, a woman named Mary McLoughlin, was on her way to visit a neighbour named Mrs Byrne when she saw what looked like statues standing in front of the southern gable end of the church. Thinking the priest had acquired them from Dublin for some purpose, she thought nothing more of it. Half an hour later Mary left Mrs Byrne's house in the company of the latter's daughter, Mary Byrne. The two women passed the church and both again saw the 'statues'. Suddenly Mary Byrne exclaimed that they were moving and identified one of the figures as the Virgin Mary. Mary Byrne ran off to tell others and soon a small group of villagers – ranging from six to seventy-six in age – had gathered to contemplate the scene. What they saw through the pouring rain were three figures, all standing about two feet off the ground. In the centre was the Virgin Mary, wearing a crown and white cloak, her hands raised, as if in prayer. To her right was St Joseph, slightly bowed in deference to the Virgin. To her left was a figure whom they took to be St John the Evangelist. He had his right hand raised, as if he were preaching, held an open book in his left hand and wore a bishop's mitre. To St John's left was an altar with a lamb standing on it in front of a cross.

The tableau was bathed in glowing light, which one witness saw from half a mile away. The figures were three-dimensional, but they did not speak and when people approached them they receded towards the gable wall. One woman, Bridget Trench, tried to kiss the feet of the Virgin but found them insubstantial; she also discovered that the ground beneath the figures was dry. None of the witnesses fell into a rapture, but all were filled with profound awe. After half an hour Mary McLoughlin went off to tell the priest, Archdeacon Cavanagh, about the wonder; but he failed to be impressed enough to go out and see it – a great irony since afterwards many locals believed they had been granted the apparition precisely because of the priest's holiness (he later fully believed in the apparition and was the first moving force at the shrine). After a while, a couple of others also departed because it was raining so hard. Then finally a woman named Judith Campbell went off to check up on her sick mother and, finding that she had collapsed, rushed back to the church to tell the others. They immediately ran over to help the woman (who died a couple of weeks later); but when they returned to the church, they found the figures had gone.

News of the apparition immediately spread through the village, then the county and the whole country. In October a Church commission examined fifteen of the witnesses and pronounced their joint testimony as 'trustworthy'. Sceptics down the years have pointed to the fact that the apparition succeeded in bringing much-needed money into the locality – that is, there was a strong economic motive for the miracle. And there were suggestions at the time that phosphorescent paint or a magic lantern might have been used to create the effect, though these were soon discounted since they failed to address the fact that the figures were three-dimensional, that the ground underneath was dry although it was raining and that the light could be seen half a mile away. Nor did the event bear the hallmarks of mass hysteria and hallucination: the witnesses were calm and lucid, and the two Marys at first interpreted the figures rationally as statues. Could it have been a pre-arranged conspiracy? Or, put another way, how would it be possible to show it had not been a conspiracy? The testimony has seemed consistently truthful to believers and sceptics alike, and the Church gave no credence to several other apparitions reported at Knock in 1880.

In any case, unofficial groups of pilgrims began arriving at Knock within weeks. Many began to chip off pieces of cement from the gable wall in the hope they would effect a cure – some dissolved them in water which they then drank. In 1882 the visiting Archishop of Toronto noted a vast number of crutches and sticks lining the gable wall – left behind by those who had apparently been cured – and an 'iron railing around the ends of the church to prevent the pilgrims from again removing the plaster from the gable'. Now the gable wall is enclosed by a glass-fronted chapel, through which a tableau of white marble statues can be seen, representing the figures of the apparition.

One of the strangest aspects of the Knock apparition was the lack of a verbal message, and speculation as to its meaning has perforce focused on the visual symbolism. The lamb on the altar, for instance, recalls the description in John's Gospel of Jesus as 'the Lamb of God, who takes away the sins of the world', as well as the image of the Lamb standing on the throne in the Book of Revelation. As such, it perhaps represents the sacrifice of Jesus and his ultimate triumph over death. Of the

other figures, Mary and Joseph conformed to traditional representations. The third figure, who looked like a bishop, was construed to be St John the Evangelist by Mary Byrne because she had seen a statue of him in a similar pose at the church of Lecanvey on the west coast of Mayo. This identification is strengthened by the fact that many believe St John wrote Revelation (which would connect him with the altar lamb) and that he looked after the Virgin Mary after the crucifixion. It might seem strange that an apparition should conform so neatly with traditional iconography. But in addressing this concern, the Church makes a distinction between what it terms 'spiritual vision' and 'interior perception'. Spiritual vision refers to glimpses of God experienced by mystics that do not involve images and can only be expressed in terms of intensity of light. Interior perception – what the Knock witnesses experienced –

ABOVE: The focus of the shrine at Knock is the 'apparition wall', where sculptures represent the figures that appeared to local parishioners in 1879.

means being able to see figures and things that are ordinarily beyond the senses: it is not fantasy but does involve the limitations of the perceivers. As Cardinal Joseph Ratzinger said in 2000, referring to the apparitions at Fatima, 'the images are, in a manner of speaking, a synthesis of the impulse coming from on high and the capacity to receive this impulse in the visionaries'.

Even if the figures can be accurately identified their significance is still open to interpretation. For example, through their various attitudes they might stand for different aspects of Christian life, such as devotion (Joseph), prayer (Mary), preaching (John) and the conquest of death (the Lamb). The connection with Revelation may also suggest that in the same way as that book was intended to hearten the persecuted Church 2,000 years ago, so the Knock apparition was meant to give hope to the desperate, downtrodden communities of pre-independence Ireland. Or perhaps the Lamb – the risen Christ – and Mary, whose crown and radiance echo the description of the woman in Revelation who is 'cloaked with the sun, with the moon under her feet, and on her head a crown of twelve stars', combine to create a cosmic image of the Church triumphant. So the 'message' might be that through the victory of Christ over death the faithful can look forward to the prospect of blessedness in heaven.

On the other hand, it may also be that theological interpretation misses the point. Certainly what struck the Knock witnesses most was the apparition's miraculous nature and its beauty – so strange and intense that it made some, including the twenty-year-old Dominick Byrne, burst into tears and left Bridget Trench with the feeling that the 'figures and the brightness would continue there always'. The youngest of the witnesses, six-year-old John Curry, told the Church authorities that he saw 'the fine images and the light, and heard the people talk of them, and went upon the wall to see the nice things and the lights'. Fifty-seven years later, in 1936, Curry was again questioned by the Church about the apparition and said that he would remember the figures 'till I go to my grave'. For believers, perhaps the point about Knock is that unlike at Lourdes, where the Virgin seemed to confirm the Church doctrine of the Immaculate Conception, or at Fatima, where the Virgin gave instructions about the rosary and divulged 'secrets', the message is simply the apparition itself, without elaboration, a grace-given glimpse of the dimension of the divine.

CROAGH PATRICK

Ireland's holiest mountain and a place of Christian pilgrimage for more than 1,500 years, Croagh Patrick rises from the southern edge of Clew Bay near the town of Westport, about thirty-five miles west of Knock. Known locally as the Reek, what makes this majestic cone-shaped mountain sacred is the pious legend that in AD 441 St Patrick spent the forty days and nights of Lent fasting on top of its peak. According to later medieval accounts in the *Book of Armagh* and the *Tripartite Life of St Patrick*, the saint was assailed during his vigil by multitudes of demonic black birds – so many that 'he knew not heaven or earth'. His attempt to drive them off with 'maledictive psalms' failed, so he resorted to striking his bell – so vigorously that it could be heard across the country – before flinging it at his assailants: 'No demon came to Ireland after that till the end of seven years and seven months and seven days and seven nights.'

By tradition Patrick also drove the poisonous snakes and other reptiles of Ireland from the mountain into the sea. That Ireland was famed for being free of reptiles was certainly well known to Bede, who wrote that 'there are no reptiles, and no snake can exist there' and that its very air would kill any such creatures on a ship approaching the country. Bede also reported that a common remedy for snakebites in England was to drink water in which 'scrapings' from Irish books had been steeped – an approach similar to that of the Knock pilgrims who drank water mixed with cement particles from the church gable. After his successful efforts to dispel the black birds, Patrick sank to the ground weeping with relief and was rewarded with the sight of a consolatory angel and a flock of melodiously singing white birds – which have been traditionally identified as the choirs of Ireland's saints, past, present and future, gathering round the saint to join him in blessing the people of Ireland.

There are scattered references to the Croagh Patrick pilgrimage in chronicles and other records down the centuries. In 1113, for example, the *Annals of Ulster* state that lightning killed thirty people fasting on top of the mountain on St Patrick's Day,

Croagh Patrick at dawn. The reputation of this remote mountain as a place of pilgrimage in Ireland rests on its historic spiritual associations with St Patrick and on its dramatic natural beauty.

17 March. In 1432 Pope Eugene IV granted an indulgence to pilgrims to the mountain. In 1652 a priest named James O'Mahony referred to the Reek pilgrimage as the most widely celebrated in the country. And in 1843, in his *Irish Sketch Book*, William Makepeace Thackeray rhapsodized about Croagh Patrick and its setting: 'The mountains were tumbled about in a thousand fantastic ways . . . but the bay, and the Reek, which sweeps down to the sea, and a hundred islands in it, were dressed up in gold and purple, and crimson with the whole cloudy west in a flame. Wonderful! Wonderful!'

Thackeray wrote his words just before the great famine that struck Ireland from 1845 to 1848, decimating the population through death and emigration – in Mayo it was reduced by at least a half. In the decades that followed, the Croagh Patrick pilgrimage declined in popularity. But in the early 1900s the Archbishop of Tuam, Dr John Healy, and a local priest named Michael McDonald set about breathing fresh life into the ancient pilgrimage. One major step was to build a new oratory on top of the mountain. There had been a chapel of some sort on the peak for as long as anyone could remember, reputedly going back to the times of Patrick (indeed, excavations in the 1990s revealed signs of settlement on and around the mountain reaching back several centuries before the Christian era). But what had survived of the chapel into the twentieth century was no longer adequate for the saying of Mass or for prayer. McDonald hired a local architect and building contractor, who erected the new sanctuary with a workforce of twelve local men, laboriously carrying bags of sand, cement and girders up the mountain by donkey, horse and hand. On 30 July 1905 the oratory was dedicated by Dr Healy at a gathering of some 10,000 pilgrims.

From that time on the pilgrimage has never looked back, with an estimated average of 30,000 souls, some barefoot, making the ascent on the last Sunday in July – Reek Sunday. Although the mountain is not particularly high (about 2,500 feet), the going can be rough over stretches of shale. The ascent begins with a long but relatively gentle climb past a welcoming statue of St Patrick to a level ridge where, the habitual mist permitting, the plains and hills of Connemara suddenly sweep into view to the south. To the north the myriad islets of Clew Bay (one, it is said, for every day of the year) break up the rippling lines of the sea like a fleet of surfacing submarines. On the ridge, devout pilgrims walk seven times around a mound of stones – the first of three stations – reciting Our Fathers, Hail Marys and the Creed. From this ridge there is a final vertiginous and arduous ascent to the very top, a small plateau where pilgrims can flop down and gaze out towards the Atlantic Ocean – or more usually a sea of white mist – or as part of the second station walk around the chapel and 'St Patrick's Bed', the traditional spot where the saint slept during his period of fasting. The final station, three mounds of stones, lies to the west of the summit.

Climbing Croagh Patrick takes a matter of hours, usually from three to five. But for many pilgrims the strain, discomfort, frequent recourse to willpower, if not prayer, and ultimate elation during that short but intense time encapsulate the highs and lows of longer pilgrimages. Unlike at Knock, where the journey has become secondary to the shrine and the practice of ritual devotion, the Croagh Patrick pilgrimage is as much about travelling as it is about arriving. It is a pilgrimage in which the natural elements – the clinging mist, the unexpected vistas of distant hills, the sea and mountains, the sudden changes from blazing blue skies to numbing grey rain, the spontaneous words of encouragement passed like batons of friendship between pilgrims – all contribute to a sense of the pilgrim experience of *communitas*, a feeling of participating together in an exhilarating spiritual enterprise.

Pilgrims following in the footsteps of St Patrick, climbing the stony path at Croagh Patrick.

FATIMA

For many Christians the so-called 'third secret' of Fatima hung over the twentieth century like the sword of Damocles. The secret was part of a message told to three illiterate children in 1917 by a figure that shone 'brighter than the sun', while they were tending sheep in fields near Fatima, seventy miles north of Lisbon. The figure, who appeared on a number of occasions, declared herself to be the Virgin Mary. Her message revealed a terrifying vision of hell and seemed to indicate that although World War I, which was currently raging in Europe, would come to an end, another great conflagration would happen in the future. There was also a specific warning that Russia (at the time convulsed by the Bolshevic Revolution) would spread its brand of atheistic Communism throughout the world, resulting in the persecution of the Church.

The message of Our Lady of Fatima (which became known as the 'first two secrets') was written down in the early 1940s by Lucia dos Santos, the only survivor of the three children, about twenty-five years after she had received it. But part of the message – the 'third secret' – she chose not to reveal, preferring to consign it to a sealed envelope which she gave to the local bishop of Leiria, who in turn passed it on to the Vatican in 1957. A number of popes read the 'third secret' but did not reveal it, prompting speculation that it was too traumatic for Christian ears. Then on 13 May 2000, Pope John Paul II, who was in Fatima to beatify Jacinta and Francisco Martos (the two children who had died soon after witnessing the Fatima apparitions) ended the suspense. The secret consisted of a vision of a 'bishop dressed in white' – the children had presumed it was the pope – passing through 'a big city half in ruins', 'afflicted with pain and sorrow' and praying for 'the souls of corpses he met on the way'. When the 'bishop' had climbed to the top of a steep mountain he kneeled down at the foot of a large cross and was killed by soldiers firing 'bullets and arrows at him'. Suggestive of the wars and atrocities of the twentieth century, the secret also held personal relevance for John Paul II, who interpreted the attack on the 'bishop' in the light of his own attempted assassination on 13 May 1981, when a Turk named

Jacinta and Francisco Martos with their cousin Lucia dos Santos (left) in 1917 after witnessing the apparition of Our Lady of Fatima. Lucia was the only one of the three children to survive into adulthood.

Mehmet Ali Agca shot him twice in St Peter's Square. The Pope afterwards attributed his survival to the 'guiding hand' of the Virgin Mary.

As with Lourdes and Knock, the genesis of Fatima as a pilgrimage place is entirely due to an apparition, or series of apparitions. And as with the other two shrines the central supernatural figure in the story is the Virgin Mary. What was it, it may be asked, that made her appear at Fatima? The town is situated in a dry, dusty, unspectacular landscape. In 1917 the area, like the rest of the country, was suffering from the hardships incurred by the Great War. As Portuguese troops joined the battlefront, farming declined, food became scarcer and prices soared. In addition, the Church was being oppressed by the Republican government, which had come to power in 1910 and was enacting anti-clerical policies, suspecting the Church of being in league with the ousted monarchist party. Fatima follows the pattern of Lourdes and Knock in that it was a place suffering from social, political and religious problems; and like the other two shrines, it has benefited materially from the thousands of pilgrims who made, and make, their way there every year. Sceptics might smile inwardly at the correlation between the miraculous and economic need; but believers could argue that it is precisely among the needy that faith is often at its strongest – with the power to attract divine grace in the form of apparitions. This, however, still does not explain what marked out Fatima (or Lourdes or Knock) as being suitable to receive an apparition, since there must have been countless other equally downtrodden places in Portugal.

The three children lived in the small village of Aljustrel, about half a mile to the south of Fatima, which in 1917 was only a hamlet. They used to graze their sheep in fields in and around a natural depression called the Cova da Iria, about a mile from Fatima. It was in this setting at about noon on 14 May 1917, a bright cloudless day, that they saw a flash of lightning and then, above a small scrubby tree, a ball of light enclosing a Lady 'dispensing light, clearer and more intense than a crystal cup full of crystalline water penetrated by the most glaring sun'. The Lady told them she was from heaven but did not disclose her name at first, instead instructing them to come back to the same spot every month for the next six months, after which she would reveal her identity. She also told the children that they would suffer because of humanity's sin, and she finished by opening her hands and letting two beams of light unfold, filling them with a sense of divine radiance.

The children kept their rendezvous with the Lady on 13 June, when they were accompanied by a small crowd of curious onlookers. Again the Lady appeared above the tree to the children (she was invisible to everyone else), and told them they must recite the rosary. She also said she would take Jacinta and Francisco to heaven very soon but that Lucia would remain on earth. By 13 July nearly three thousand people had gathered to watch as the children saw the Lady return, bathing them, as they felt, in radiant light and revealing her message to them. Matters went awry on 13 August, when the children were snatched away to the town of Ourém by the hostile local Republican administrator, who tried to force them to reveal the Lady's message. Despite threats of being boiled alive in oil the children said nothing and were released. Although they missed their meeting with the Lady, she did appear six days later and said she would perform a miracle at her last appearance 'so that all shall believe'.

By 13 September the crowd was bigger than ever and included a number of high-ranking priests, who had come to observe what by now was a well-publicized phenomenon. As at Lourdes and Knock the Church was cautious, wishing neither to alienate the thousands, mostly peasants, who believed in the children nor to appear superstitious and gullible, and thereby play into the hands of their enemies. This time some of the crowd claimed to see a 'globe of light' slowly move towards them, but not the Lady herself, whom only the children saw. She told them to keep saying the rosary and reassured them that next month she would perform a public miracle.

On 13 October, there were an estimated 70,000 people gathered in the rain at the Cova. The midday deadline came and went. Then out of the grey skies the Lady appeared to the children in a flood of white light, and announced to them that she was the Lady of the Rosary and that a chapel must be built in her honour. The children also saw St Joseph, the Child Jesus and other representations of the Lady: grieving as Our Lady of Sorrows; then crowned as the Queen of Heaven. Then the crowd witnessed the promised miracle: the sun appeared as a bright silver disk and began to 'dance' – spinning like a Catherine wheel, flinging out streams of flame, and bathing the earth in the colours of the rainbow. Then it seemed to vibrate and plummet, zigzagging towards the onlookers. People fell to their knees in swathes, crying aloud in terror or bursting into tears, thinking the world was coming to an end. Then just as suddenly the orb began to withdraw to the sky and resumed its ordinary place as the sun. The

'miracle' has remained a mystery. Sceptics and atheists saw it; hostile Republican newspapers described it; and individuals who were not expecting anything spotted it from up to thirty miles away. Some of the crowd, it must be said, did not see it. But thousands did. There was no suggestion of the event being an eclipse or any other measurable astronomical phenomenon, and it still remains baffling to those who wish to interpret it rationally. For believers, there were few precedents for what happened. It is highly unlikely that anyone there knew that a nineteenth-century Scottish folklorist, Alexander Carmichael, had recorded the vision of a woman named Barbara Macphie, seen from a hill in Scotland at Easter: 'the glorious gold-bright sun . . . rising on the crests of the great hills, and it was changing colour – green, purple, red, blood-red, white, intense white, and gold-white, like the glory of God of the elements to the children of men. It was dancing up and down in exultation at the joyous resurrection of the beloved Saviour of victory.' Unlike Macphie's joyful vision, however, the Fatima sun seems to have provoked mainly fears of catastrophe and doom.

Boosted by the extraordinary apparitions and, in 1930, by the formal endorsement of the Church, Fatima grew as a place of pilgrimage and became established as one of the foremost shrines in the world, especially after World War II, when hotels, hostels and other facilities were built for the annual surge of pilgrims between May and October. The touristy atmosphere and the perfunctory architecture of the basilica, are alleviated by the torchlit processions, the small Chapel of the Apparitions, where candles commemorate the spot where the Lady appeared, and the moment when women wave their white handkerchiefs, like so many wings of doves, as the statue of Our Lady is borne aloft around the basilica square. Whereas Lourdes is associated with healing, the key note at Fatima is penance, the consciousness of sin and the need for reparation in order to avert a global disaster. This warning from the Lady, coupled with the apocalyptic sign of the 'dancing sun', seems to suit the mentality of the nuclear age. At Lourdes the magnetic centre is the small, intimate earthly grotto; at Fatima it is difficult not to keep looking up at the sun.

A crowd of pilgrims at the shrine of Our Lady of Fatima. Over four million people visit the sanctuary each year. There are special pilgrimage services held on the 13th day of each month.

WALSINGHAM

Apart from the rise of new shrines such as Lourdes, Knock and Fatima, the late nineteenth and early twentieth centuries saw the revival of some medieval places of pilgrimage, if not a return to the cult of saints and relics. These revived shrines draw upon their centuries-old spiritual inheritance; and they now also attract pilgrims concerned with contemporary Christian issues, such as social welfare, ecology and the unity of the Church. Although these sites may have lost some of the intensity and mystery of yesteryear, they have undoubtedly gained a new popularity through their greater informality and openness.

In the Middle Ages, Walsingham, near the north coast of Norfolk, was second only to Canterbury as England's greatest pilgrim destination. It was the home of the shrine known as the 'Holy House', said to have been modelled on the house of the Virgin at Nazareth. Walsingham came to grief in 1538 during the Reformation, and the towering priory to which the shrine was attached became a ruin (only one elegant arch now remains). As visitors ceased to come, what was once a thriving pilgrimage centre dwindled to a place with a fading past and no future. According to an anonymous Elizabethan ballad: 'Owls do scrike where the sweetest hymns lately were sung,/Toads and serpents hold their dens where the palmers did throng./Weep, weep, O Walsingham, whose days are nights,/Blessings turned to blasphemies, holy deeds to despites.'

In the late nineteenth century, however, the blasphemies began to turn back to blessings. Walsingham's revival began in 1894, when a devout Anglican named Charlotte Boyd bought and restored the dilapidated medieval Slipper Chapel, which stands about a mile from the main shrine. Its name may come from the pilgrims' practice of taking off their shoes there before walking the last part of the way barefooted. Boyd then converted to the Catholic faith and presented the chapel to the Benedictine Order, under whom it became the national Catholic shrine to Our Lady. In 1897, the first Catholic pilgrimage to Walsingham for some 350 years took place, from the Norfolk town of King's Lynn to the Slipper Chapel.

The remains of the priory on the site of the original shrine at Walsingham, Norfolk. Although the shrine and its relics have long since been lost, the site has again become one of the most important pilgrimage destinations in Europe.

In the 1920s the Church of England joined in the spirit of revival when the local vicar, Revd Alfred Hope Patten, provided a focus for Anglican pilgrimage by installing a new statue of Our Lady (based on an image on the priory's medieval seal) in the parish church. In 1931 a new Anglican shrine, consisting of a small church enclosing a replica of the Holy House, was built opposite the ruins of the priory, and the statue was duly translated from the parish church. In the following years both Catholics and Anglicans continued to respond to the revival, and once again 'sweet hymns' were sung in the streets as pilgrims processed through Walsingham to the different shrines.

Walsingham traditionally became a shrine in 1061, shortly before the Norman invasion of England. In that year, a local well-to-do widow named Richelde de Faverches received a vision of the Virgin Mary, who revealed to her the house in Nazareth where the Annunciation had taken place and where the Holy Family had lived after the birth of Jesus. The vision of the Holy House was repeated two more times, and the Virgin instructed Richeldis to memorize its dimensions and to build a replica on her estate. Richeldis was not sure where to locate the shrine, until one morning she woke to see what she interpreted as a divine sign: on one of her fields were two rectangular dry patches in the heavy dew. Having to choose between the two spots, she told her workmen to raise the wooden structure on the one nearest two wells. But as hard as they tried the builders could not get their structure to fit the space. Disgruntled after a day of frustration, they left their tools and materials on the ground and went off home. That night Richeldis prayed for guidance, and as she did so the Virgin and her angels erected the house on the other patch – much to the astonishment of the workers when they discovered it next morning.

The Walsingham story echoes the pattern and motifs of other Christian foundation legends, for example that of St Mary the Greater in Rome, built on the spot where snow miraculously fell during the summer; or the Holy House of Loreto, near Ancona in Italy, which was said to have been transported by angels from Nazareth to Italy (via Dalmatia) in 1295. There is also the story of the Dark Age Welsh saint Brannock, who struggled to build a church in the north of Devon at what is now the town of Braunton, until he received a vision in which an angel told him to build where he saw a sow suckling her piglets. Shortly afterwards Brannock saw the sow on a meadow near a stream and duly built his church there. The point about these traditions is that they emphasize the grace-given origins of the shrines, and that human ingenuity and craftsmanship can never be of the same order as divine creation.

Walsingham's Holy House gradually became famous throughout the land. At a time when Europe's finest sons were going off to Palestine on Crusade or pilgrimage, the Holy House served for many people as a substitute, a small corner of the Holy Land tucked away in rural East Anglia. Down the centuries, to the time of Henry VIII and its dissolution, the shrine was well patronized by kings, queens and nobles, becoming prosperous from various gifts of land, money and jewels. Pilgrims came from all over the country and from abroad: those arriving from the south travelled by way of Newmarket, Swaffham and Fakenham, while those from the north tended to gather at King's Lynn before walking the last twenty-odd miles east to Walsingham. All along these routes hostels and wayside chapels catered for the pilgrim bands, which included, according to a fifteenth-century ballad, the blind, the lame, the deaf and lepers, as well as, according to the fourteenth-century poet William Langland, 'false hermits' who 'went to Walsingham with their wenches after'.

The climax of the journey was a visit to the priory and the chapel that contained the Holy House, which when Erasmus visited it (see pages 130–31) was a small wooden construction with a door on each side to allow for the constant flow of pilgrims. It was dark, sweet-smelling and lit only by tapers that made the offerings of gold, silver and gemstones glitter. It also had an altar and a statue of the Virgin – undistinguished, Erasmus thought, in size, material and craftsmanship, but 'most efficacious in virtue'. The other main object of devotion in the priory was a glass phial allegedly containing drops of the Virgin's milk. Another stop for pilgrims, especially the infirm, was the priory's two wells and sunken bath, where they could bathe or drink the holy water – which was recommended for headaches and heartburn – or collect some to take back home in a flask. After the Reformation, the wells became 'wishing' wells – a secular transformation known to have happened to other holy wells, such as St Margaret's Well at Binsey in Oxfordshire.

Walsingham drew pilgrims for nearly 500 years until the suppression of the monasteries by Henry VIII. Ironically, the king had been devoted to the shrine earlier in his reign. He made the first pilgrimage there as king on 19 January 1511, and afterwards donated a ruby-encrusted collar and money to glaze the windows of the shrine chapel; and in the royal accounts there are entries up to 1538 recording the annual donation to the shrine of the 'King's Candle' and the services of a priest to sing before the statue of Our Lady. A visit in 1536 from royal commissioners, intent on reporting on Walsingham's affairs and preparing the way for its dissolution, fired the first warning shots across the shrine's bow. During their investigations the men found 'a secret privy place' in which were strange instruments, pots and potions with which to 'divide gold and silver' – implying a secret mint or an alchemist's laboratory. In fact it was almost certainly just a workshop for casting pilgrims' medals and souvenirs. The end finally came on 4 August 1538, when the shrine was formally surrendered to the Crown. The entry from the king's accounts for 29 September of the same year sums up Walsingham's sudden change of status: 'For the King's Candle before Our Lady of Walsingham, and to the Prior there for his salary – Nil.' The statue of Our Lady was burned. The priory was sold to a private family, and its church, stripped of lead and pillaged for stone, soon collapsed. As the Elizabethan ballad expressed it: 'Bitter, bitter oh to behold the grass to grow/Where the walls of Walsingham so stately did show'.

Now the cycle of history has turned again and the Walsingham Way, the main pilgrimage trail whose name was once used to describe the Milky Way, resounds again with the tread of pilgrims' feet, as bands of Catholics and Anglicans process to the shrines. For Catholics the focus of pilgrimage is the Slipper Chapel. Inside the small, high-roofed medieval structure the interior has been restored and modern windows put in, including a stained-glass depiction of the Annunciation, installed in 1997 to mark the centenary of the revived pilgrimage. The modern statue of Our Lady, which shows the Virgin with the Christ Child on her knee, was blessed by Pope John Paul II during a mass held at Wembly Stadium in 1982. For Anglicans the climax of the pilgrimage is their modern shrine, several yards to the north of the old priory wall. This stone and red-brick structure houses a replica of the Holy House, inside which the visitor steps back into a medieval atmosphere of dim light, flickering candles, a glittering altar, and the statue of the Crowned Virgin, wrapped in an embroidered cape that is taken off, along with her crown, at the start of Advent and Lent. The Reformers could destroy the structure but not the memory of the shrine's devotions; and the memory has been restored to the extent that even Erasmus, the gentle mocker of pilgrimage, would surely recognize it.

IONA

The tiny island of Iona off the west coast of Scotland, now home to a spiritual community founded in 1938 by Reverend George MacLeod, has been a place of informal pilgrimage since the days of the Irish saint Columba, who founded a monastery there in 563. During the Dark Ages, Iona became famous for producing dedicated monks and missionaries, who journeyed to mainland Britain to convert pagans, strengthen the Faith and establish other monasteries, such as Lindisfarne in northeast England. After his death, Columba was buried on Iona and his body remained there until the Viking raids of the early 800s, when his bones were taken off to safety in Ireland. So although Columba is forever linked with Iona, there was never a cult there based around a tomb or a shrine of the sort that occurred in the later Middle Ages, as at Canterbury for example. In a way the saint's shrine is Iona itself, with its natural jewels: emerald fields, golden beaches, amethyst heather.

What has undoubtedly helped to revive the popularity of Columba and his island in the twentieth and early twenty-first centuries is their association with contemporary 'Celtic Christianity'. This somewhat blanket term refers to an increasingly popular approach to Christianity, involving more informal ways of worship and emphasizing the natural world and human creativity – celebrating the divine through music, dance, painting and writing. Columba fits this ideal well: he himself was not only a mystic and a lover of nature but also an assiduous copyist of manuscripts as well as a poet. According to the medieval Old Irish *Life* of the saint, his writing fingers 'were as candles which shone like five bright lamps'; and there are a number of ancient Irish poems attributed to Columba which, although mostly dating from later times, at least suggest he had a reputation for writing about God and nature – a world of birdsong and wild winds and seas. Over time the island itself has gained a reputation for inspiring artists and other free spirits, although there are no great monuments for the heart and mind to respond to – only a small, restored medieval abbey and a scattering of hallowed ruins. The very lack of an overwhelming shrine frees the imagination, allowing it to rove over Iona's landscape and its many connections with Columban legends. In short, what Iona has is atmosphere. The barely expressible sense a visitor has of being on a different spiritual plane moved even the habitually down-to-earth Dr Samuel Johnson, who first set foot on the island in

1773, to declare: 'That man is little to be envied, whose patriotism would not gain force upon the plain of Marathon, or whose piety would not grow warmer among the ruins of Iona.' The island inspired both John Keats and William Wordsworth to write about it after visits there in 1818 and 1835 respectively; and Felix Mendelssohn, in a letter from Glasgow dated August 1829, wrote that in 'some future time I shall sit in a madly crowded assembly with music and dancing round me . . . I shall think of Iona with its ruins of a once magnificent cathedral, the remains of a convent, the graves of ancient Scottish kings.'

Mendelssohn and Sir Walter Scott (whose Highland tour in the summer of 1810 included Iona) both found melancholy among the beauties of the island, with Scott remarking on the wretchedness of the inhabitants. In fact the island had been in steady decline since 1561, when the medieval Benedictine abbey built on the site of Columba's original monastery was dismantled by order of the Reformation authorities. The buildings gradually disintegrated and the island passed into lay hands, at first the Macleans and then, in 1693, the Campbells. The revival of Iona's fortunes began in 1874, when restoration was started on the abbey church. Then in 1899 the chief of the Campbells, the eighth Duke of Argyll, returned the abbey to the care of religious authorities by donating it to the Church of Scotland.

Nearly forty years later, in 1938, a minister in the Church of Scotland named George MacLeod founded the Iona Community – an event that has perhaps done more than anything to put post-Reformation Iona back on the spiritual map. Brought up in a wealthy family in Glasgow, MacLeod joined the Church of Scotland after serving in World War I, a traumatic experience that made him determined to help the victims of society. Working in a severely underprivileged area of Glasgow, MacLeod set about trying to help the poor, the unemployed and others whom he felt society had failed. It was to implement his ideas on social justice and action that he founded the Iona Community. With the help of thousands of volunteers he restored the abbey and made it the heart of an ecumenical Christian community, as well as a centre for retreats and programmes of spiritual renewal. The community now has about 250

In front of the west door of the restored medieval Iona Abbey stands a Celtic cross dedicated to the fourth-century French bishop St Martin.

members who live throughout Britain and are committed to a rule that involves 'a daily devotional discipline, sharing and accounting for their use of time and money, regular meeting and action for justice and peace'. Following the lead of MacLeod, who died in 1991, the community continues to emphasize issues such as social justice, economic action to alleviate poverty and ecological concerns.

This stress on worldly matters may seem a far cry from the mystical, nature-loving figure of Columba depicted by his medieval biographers. But in fact the community's religious perspective fully reflects the dynamic, practical side of the saint – a side that is often overlooked. Though deeply spiritual, Columba could also be a hard-nosed, energetic man of the world, as little squeamish about getting involved in local politics as he was ardent in his vigils and devotions to God.

ABOVE: Port a'Chuvaich ('The Harbour of the Coracle'), where St Columba first landed on Iona after his departure from Ireland in 563.

Columba was born in Donegal, northwest Ireland, in 521. With a family tree that included Niall of the Nine Hostages, high king of Ireland in the late fourth century, Columba grew up into a confident, able and determined man of God. He founded his first monastery at Derry when he was in his mid-twenties, followed by others some years later at Durrow, Kells and elsewhere. The turning point of his life came in 563, when he set sail from Ireland, 'desiring to seek a foreign country for the sake of Christ', as his seventh-century biographer Adomnan recorded – indicating that Columba was behaving in the manner of a typical Irish *peregrinus*. Another tradition, however, suggests that he was actually exiled by the Church for his role in igniting a battle between two rival branches of the Uí Neill tribe. For his alleged part in this affair, Columba was ordered by the Church authorities to convert as many pagans as the number of Irishmen killed in the fighting.

Whatever the reason for his departure, Columba set sail from Ireland with twelve companions and settled on Iona – the first landfall, so the story goes, from which he could not look back and see his beloved country. On Iona the monks set about creating their monastery, building huts with wood and wattle, erecting a solid, oaken church, sowing crops and hunting seals for food and lamp oil. Once established, the Irish brethren were ready to move eastwards and begin their mission to convert the pagans on the mainland. At this time what is now Scotland was split into different political areas, notably Dalriada, a kingdom in the west founded by Irish settlers (who were known as 'Scots', the name later applied to all the inhabitants of the country); and the regions of the Picts, which covered most of the country north of the Firth of Forth.

Little is known about the Picts. They were probably descendants of Scotland's Iron Age tribes, and their name ('painted ones') suggests they painted or tattooed their bodies. Their society seems to have been hierarchical, with a king at the top and soldiers, priests, craftsmen and peasants below him. The Picts may have encountered Christianity before Columba's arrival, through earlier missionaries and trading contacts with England and Ireland; but it was the endeavours of Columba that posterity remembers, honouring him as the father of Scottish Christianity. Like Columbanus (see pages 42–4), his younger contemporary, Columba had no fear of kings and according to Adomnan he made Brude, the ruler of the northern Picts, his first major target for conversion. Travelling up the Great Glen to Brude's stronghold at Inverness, the saint found the gates of the palace locked against him. Nothing daunted, he made the sign of the cross and the gates flew open, a feat that so impressed the king he converted to Christianity.

Much has to be inferred about Columba's missionary work from the few details that remain; he must be imagined making frequent sorties from Iona, impressing Pictish chiefs with his unshakeable faith and personal confidence, challenging pagan Druid priests to trials of spiritual strength, organizing converts, and acting as a counsellor and diplomat to local rulers. After bouts of fervent activity he would retreat to Iona and devote himself to the monastic life, praying, contemplating, copying manuscripts, welcoming guests, and guiding his brethren and organizing the practicalities of their existence. He was also, Adomnan records, a seer and mystic, able to predict the future – whether the spilling of an inkpot or the arrival of a pilgrim – and to encounter the divine. On one occasion a monk was said to have watched the saint converse with angels on one of the island's small hillocks. Robed in white the angels flew through the air at great speed and gathered round the saint as he prayed. Then, feeling that they were being watched, they returned to heaven. Adomnan also emphasizes the brilliant light that Columba's body would sometimes emit – as, for example, when a monk named Colga saw the monastic church in which the saint was praying 'filled with heavenly light, which more quickly than he could tell, flashed like lightning from his gaze'.

According to Adomnan, Iona was the scene of many miracles; and as pilgrims have remarked down the ages, it is a place that gives you a feeling that something extraordinary could happen. The eighth Duke of Argyll referred to the island's 'atmosphere of miracle', and George MacLeod said that the division between the material and the spiritual on Iona was only 'paper thin'. It is perhaps most of all this indefinable quality – the feeling that when you set foot on its shores you are sloughing off a skin of materialism – that now draws pilgrims to the island in greater numbers than at any other time in its history.

TAIZÉ

In 1940, over a thousand years after the Burgundian abbey of Cluny did much to reinvigorate the Church, a French-Swiss monk named Brother Roger founded in the nearby village of Taizé an ecumenical Christian community that has evolved into one of the most thriving movements in Western Christendom. Taizé's emphasis on Christian unity, its non-authoritarian approach to religion and its simple, melodic and catchy songs and prayers are particularly attractive to younger Christians. Sleeping in dormitories or in tents pitched in fields around the village, and helping with daily practicalities such as cleaning or preparing food, thousands of pilgrims, mainly aged under thirty, experience the Taizé perspective on Christianity each year. They attend the thrice-daily prayer meetings, participate in discussion groups, meditate in silence, sing together in the candlelit interior of the vast, modern Chapel of Reconciliation, and listen to talks on the Bible given by the brothers. Taizé is as much a way of life as it is a pilgrimage destination. During their stay visitors are encouraged to absorb its values, such as tolerance and fruitful introspection, and then to return home to put them into action. Taizé practises what it preaches: a number of its hundred or so brothers live abroad in the poorest parts of Africa, Asia and the Americas, attempting to relate their vision of Christianity to the people around them.

Taizé's heart and soul, Brother Roger, was born Roger Schutz-Marsauche in 1915, the son of a Protestant pastor. He grew up in a family that placed great value on charitable works and music. One major influence on Roger was his grandmother, who had turned her home in northern France into a place of refuge for the old, infirm and destitute during World War I. Other formative experiences included boarding with a Catholic family during his time at secondary school; convalescing from tuberculosis, which gave him time to study and think about his life; and becoming president of the Student Christian Federation at Lausanne University, a position that enabled him to hone his organizational skills.

By 1940, just after the outbreak of World War II, Roger was ready to put his ideas into action. Conscious of the sufferings of the defeated French people, he decided to take a leaf out of his grandmother's book and establish a house that would serve as a place of prayer and of practical assistance for refugees and local people devastated by the war. Leaving Geneva on his bicycle, he crossed into eastern France to buy a

suitable house. His quest ended at Taizé, at that time a semi-derelict village with a dirt track for a road and no running water or telephone. While viewing a house for sale he was struck by the words of an old woman who implored him: 'Stay here with us; we are so poor and isolated.' The die was cast. Within several weeks Roger had bought the house, created a small chapel, cleared the surrounding land and was even milking his own cow. Soon refugees began to arrive, many of them Jews. (Roger would go off into the woods to pray in order not to offend their religious sensibilities.) In 1942, however, the Nazis got wind of the refuge and closed it down. Roger happened to be in Switzerland at the time, trying to raise money, and was forced to stay there until 1944. In that year he returned to Taizé with a small group of Christian friends, intent on establishing a monastic community based on traditional Christian virtues and on helping those uprooted by war – a tradition which has continued. In the 1990s, for example, Taizé gave shelter to families affected by fighting in the Balkans.

In 1949 seven more brothers joined the community, which continued to evolve along non-denominational lines. By the 1960s there were Taizé brothers from Reformed, Lutheran and Anglican traditions. Then in 1969 the first Catholic joined the community – a momentous occasion for which the ground had been prepared eleven years previously by a meeting between Roger and the reforming Pope John XXIII, who later expressed his warmth towards the community with the words, 'Ah, Taizé, that little springtime!' This sentiment was later echoed by Pope John Paul II in an address to the community in 1986, when he told them that 'One passes through Taizé as one passes close to a spring of water. The traveller stops, quenches his thirst and continues on his way.'

This idea of taking spiritual refreshment from Taizé and using it elsewhere to good effect informs one of the community's central programmes – what it calls 'a pilgrimage of trust on earth'. The basic premise for this is that people should combine personal inner pilgrimage – which, as Roger has written, involves 'visiting with Christ each of our own prisons [to] see some of the walls fall down [and] spaces of freedom open up' – with external action. It is a commitment to lead an active Christian life in the local community. There are no strict rules about how to conduct this 'pilgrimage of trust'

The small and unostentatious village of Taizé, Burgundy,
with the brothers' residence in the foreground.

– that would be contrary to Taizé's informal ethos. Nevertheless, there are two annual events that aim to provide stimulation and encouragement. The first is the publication of an open letter by Roger – usually written during a stay in one of the world's poorest regions – which crystallizes his thoughts about certain religious themes that serve as a focus of reflection for the following year. The second is the 'European Meeting', organized by the brothers with the help of local volunteers, at which tens of thousands of young adults from all over the world gather at a major European city (destinations have included Prague, London, Warsaw and Barcelona) for several days to take part in prayers, services, retreats, communal singing and workshops. The aim is for Christians from different backgrounds and walks of life to share ideas, problems and perceptions and to take home with them a renewed sense of purpose and vitality.

Why Taizé has proved to be so popular at a time when many churches in the West are in decline is difficult to pinpoint. Its success may be due to a combination of its simple but affecting liturgy, its ability to balance seriousness with informality and its tolerance of Christian diversity yet tight focus on the Gospel and core Christian values. Above all, rather than laying down the law Taizé invites self-exploration in a gentle, humane way, encouraging this delving to manifest itself in positive, practical ways in the sphere of social action, thereby striking a balance between the active and reflective modes of Christianity. Another significant factor is that Taizé does not compete with other churches, who, on the contrary, seem to welcome its approach as a way of revitalizing their own traditions. As Dr George Carey, Archbishop of Canterbury, said in 1992, before leading a party of 1,000 young Anglicans there on pilgrimage, Taizé is 'a place for the seeker after truth, the searcher after God, and in this life our Christian pilgrimage is never complete'.

ABOVE: Brother Roger in Taizé, 1962; RIGHT: Owing to the large number of pilgrims to Taizé at Easter, services are held in a tent added on to the church.

EPILOGUE

At the end of this survey it remains to ask briefly what direction Christian pilgrimage will take in the future. Pilgrimage has never operated in a vacuum, and its fate is linked with the prevailing attitudes of society and the state of Christianity. Although many churches in the West are more or less in decline, pilgrimage, with or without secular adjuncts such as sightseeing or keeping fit, continues to thrive. Even for those in whom the spiritual flame is barely flickering there are secular outlets for what the religiously inclined would think of as a pilgrimage instinct. For example, as some anthropologists have noted, theme parks such as Disney World can be interpreted as a quasi-religious place of pilgrimage: 'pilgrims' travel to a world of heightened sensation where they can forget their everyday concerns; they enjoy a sense of togetherness with other pilgrims, perform various 'rituals' by joining in set activities, buy souvenir 'badges' commemorating their experience, then rejoin the world outside. Another secular outlet that may possibly become popular in the future is space travel. In May 2001, Dennis Tito, a sixty-year-old Californian multi-millionaire, became the world's first 'space tourist' when he spent a week on board the International Space Station (ISS), orbiting more than 230 miles above the Earth. His trip bears comparison with a typical pilgrimage experience: a demanding journey; arrival at the space station 'shrine'; the ecstatic fulfilment of what Tito called his 'dream'; his return home to literal 'mundanity' and verdict that he 'just came back from paradise'.

For believers, another means of making a pilgrimage has presented itself through the Internet. 'Virtual pilgrimage' is now a relatively common phenomenon. Places such as Jerusalem, Walsingham, Croagh Patrick and Taizé are accessible through websites that offer virtual journeys, sometimes accompanied by music, prayers, sacred texts, purchasable souvenirs and links to other sites. It has been argued that through virtual pilgrimage it is possible to enter the transitional state that is characteristic of physical pilgrimage – that in cyberspace net navigators can be dislocated from their environment and taken to a sacred realm, accompanied by other net pilgrims with whom they can share their experiences through guestbooks. But although virtual pilgrimage may work as a meditational aid to inner pilgrimage, the common sense objection to it is that is essentially mediated pilgrimage. The pilgrim participates through images and material of someone else's making; and unlike 'real' physical pilgrimage, which involves time in which to reflect and digest, virtual pilgrimage must induce states of inner transformation through the instantaneity of mouse-clicks. In the twelfth century Pope Alexander III referred to pilgrims journeying so that 'in the sweat of their brow and labour of the road, they may avoid the wrath of the heavenly Judge and earn his mercy'. Although pilgrimage now seldom reflects the full penitential import of the pope's words, it is difficult to disconnect it entirely from physical effort.

Despite fluctuations in its popularity, Christian pilgrimage has survived more than two thousand years and the indications are that it will continue to thrive in the future – if only because the symbolism of pilgrimage is rooted in the journey of life itself. As the Russian writer Maxim Gorky said in his play *The Lower Depths*, 'All of us are pilgrims on this earth, I have even heard people say that the earth itself is a pilgrim in the heavens'. In short, in as much as pilgrimage, with its physical effort and opportunity for spiritual reflection, mirrors the condition of humanity, it is difficult to imagine a future when people will not be setting off on journeys around the world in the search, conscious or unconscious, for help or meaning or peace or God.

GAZETTEER

Apart from the places of pilgrimage covered in the main body of this book, there are many other Christian shrines that continue to attract pilgrims from all over the world. The following are some of the better known of these.

CHIMAYÓ, UNITED STATES

Founded by Spanish colonists in the late seventeenth century, the village of Chimayó lies in a valley about twenty-seven miles north of Santa Fe in New Mexico. Some 300,000 pilgrims a year visit its small nineteenth-century adobe church, known as El Santuario and dubbed the 'Lourdes of America'. The story goes that on Good Friday in about 1810 a local friar was outside performing penances when he saw light flashing from the ground of a nearby hill. Going to investigate, he began to dig at the spot with his hands and unearthed a crucifix. On three occasions a priest from Santa Fe tried to install the crucifix in the town. But each time the crucifix mysteriously returned to the place of its discovery – so it was decided to build a chapel to house it there. This building was replaced by a larger shrine in 1816, in response to the growing number of pilgrims who came to see the crucifix, still located on the altar as it had been in the original chapel. Many came in the hope of a cure, since the earth on which the shrine was built is believed to have healing powers. Pilgrims are allowed to take away bags of sacred earth from a small room inside the church; and many have left reminders of their cure in the form of crutches, photographs and votive candles.

CZĘSTOCHOWA, POLAND

The industrial town of Częstochowa may seem an unlikely site for Poland's greatest shrine. Iron, steel and chemical plants form its economic core; but its spiritual centre is the monastery – named Jasna Gora ('Shining Mountain') after the hill it is built upon – which houses the famous icon of the Virgin Mary known as the Black Madonna. This image, traditionally painted by St Luke, may be a copy of an ancient Byzantine icon. It arrived at Jasna Gora in the Middle Ages and became nationally revered after 1655, when the monastery withstood a siege by a powerful Swedish army, inspiring a successful counterattack by the Poles. The Polish king John Casimir then dedicated the country to the Virgin Mary, recognizing the monastery and the icon as its sacred centre. Since then, the shrine has survived another attack by the Swedes, in 1702, the partition of the country, World War II and Communist rule. Now each year hundreds of thousands make the trek to Jasna Gora, many walking the 180-mile route from Warsaw to arrive in time for the feast of the Assumption on 15 August or the feast of Our Lady of Jasna Gora on 26 August. In the small chapel of the Black Madonna in Jasna Gora pilgrims pay their devotions to the icon, which for Poles fuses spirituality with patriotism.

GARABANDAL, SPAIN

Lying about thirty-five miles southwest of Santander in northern Spain, the village of Garabandal might have gained the fame and prosperity of shrines such as Fatima and Lourdes if the Church had formally recognized the numerous apparitions that four girls claimed to see there from 1961 to 1965. The apparitions were mostly of the Virgin Mary. When she appeared to the girls they would be seen to fall into an ecstasy, sometimes for hours on end. They would also offer objects such as bibles, rosaries and crucifixes – given to them by friends and pilgrims – for the Virgin to kiss. The latter would talk about everyday things such as haymaking, as well as imparting formal messages addressed to the world. These contained stern warnings about the need for sacrifice, penance and going to Mass. On one occasion the Virgin promised one of the girls, Conchita, that at some time in the future a great miracle would happen at Garabandal. This would be preceded by a 'warning' that would be seen worldwide. The last message was received in June 1965, and since then pilgrimage there has been low-key. The village's spiritual epicentre is a low hill crowned by a group of pines, where many of the apparitions occurred and where Conchita was seen to receive the Host, seemingly miraculously, on her tongue.

LOUGH DERG, IRELAND

St Patrick's Purgatory on Station Island in Lough Derg, County Donegal, is one of the most demanding pilgrimages in Europe. It lasts three days and involves fasting and a twenty-four-hour vigil during which worshippers must stay awake continuously.

During their time on the island, pilgrims perform nine 'stations', or prayer sequences. They do five of these out in the open, with bare feet, on the so-called 'penitential beds' – the stony remains of ancient monastic cells. The other four stations are performed inside the octagonal basilica that was completed in 1930. Only three meals, consisting of dry toast and black tea, are allowed throughout the three-day period. For those who feel unable to endure this regimen, there has been a one-day retreat available since 1992.

St Patrick's Purgatory is thought to have been a place of pilgrimage for more than 1,500 years. In the Middle Ages it became well known throughout Europe after an Irish-born knight named Owen wrote about his vigil there, during which he encountered the devil and was granted a glimpse of heaven. The pilgrimage survived suppression by the English government in the seventeenth century and began to revive steadily from the early part of the twentieth, since when it has never looked back.

MEDJUGORJE, BOSNIA

The village of Medjugorje in Bosnia has been a major Christian pilgrimage site since 1981, when six young adults received apparitions of the Virgin Mary there. What is unusual about Medjugorje is that the Virgin still appears on a regular basis to some of the original witnesses. Her messages focus on five themes: repentance, conversion, prayer, penance and fasting. Although situated in the war-torn Balkans, Medjugorje has the reputation of being a place of reconciliation – for Christians and Muslims, for Croats, Serbs and Bosnians, and for individuals at war with themselves. Many have remarked upon the 'Medjugorje effect' – a state of blissful peace unexpectedly experienced after staying there.

Pilgrims concentrate their devotions around the local parish Church of St James; the Hill of Apparitions, where the young witnesses first saw the Virgin, or the 'Gospa' as she is known; and neighbouring Mount Krizevac, marked by a large cement cross raised in 1934, where people have claimed to see miraculous displays of light, including the sun 'dancing'. The combination of apocalyptic messages and reports of a 'dancing sun' makes Medjugorje resemble Fatima; another similarity is that the Virgin has entrusted a number of 'secrets' to the original witnesses, who say they will reveal them at some point in the future.

Our Lady of Guadelupe, Mexico

The Basilica of Our Lady of Guadelupe in Mexico City is visited by millions of pilgrims every year, especially on the feast day of 12 December, when plumed Aztec dancers fill the plaza outside the church with movement and colour. The principal focus of the pilgrimage is a piece of cloth housed in the church, which is believed to have been miraculously imprinted with an image of the Virgin Mary. According to tradition, in 1531 an Indian peasant named Juan Diego received an apparition of the Virgin on Tepeyac Hill, now a suburb of Mexico City. The Virgin told Juan to go to the local bishop and ask him to build a chapel on the place where she had appeared. At first the bishop was sceptical and demanded to see a 'sign'. Juan reported back to the Virgin, who directed him to a rocky spot where he found some beautiful scented roses, blooming out of season. Juan gathered these up in his cloak and took them to the bishop. The latter was amazed to see not only the flowers but also, as they tumbled from Juan's cloak, an image of the Virgin imprinted on the material. In due course a church was built in the Virgin's honour and the cloak installed inside it. This was later transferred to a new basilica, built in the 1970s after the land underneath its predecessor began to subside. In 1990, Juan Diego was beatified by Pope John Paul II.

Sainte Anne de Beaupré, Canada

Situated about twenty miles northeast of Quebec along the St Lawrence River, Sainte Anne de Beaupré is the home of one of Canada's great Christian shrines and a place of pilgrimage since 1658. The story goes that a group of French sailors built the first shrine in gratitude to St Anne – the mother of the Virgin Mary – for saving their lives after they were shipwrecked on the river. During construction of the shrine, a local man named Louis Guimont was miraculously cured of rheumatism, so beginning a tradition of healing that continues to this day, as the presence of numerous crutches and walking sticks at the entrance of the shrine testifies. During the second half of the nineteenth century the number of pilgrims steadily increased, and a larger church was built in 1876. This burned down in 1922 and was replaced by the current basilica, designed as a medieval cathedral with Romanesque arches and twin steeples. In the vast interior, which can hold 9,000 worshippers, precious devotional objects include a gaily painted statue of St Anne and a relic of her arm, encased in gold.

SELECT BIBLIOGRAPHY

Adair, John *The Pilgrim's Way* London, 1978

Adamnan *Life of St Columba* (ed. W. Reeves) Edmonston and Douglas, 1874

Alexander, H.G. *Religion in England 1558–1662* London, 1968

Bede *A History of the English Church and People* Harmondsworth, 1955

Birch, Debra J. *Pilgrimage to Rome in the Middle Ages* Woodbridge, 1998

Brown, Peter *The Cult of Saints* London, 1981

Bunyan, John *The Pilgrim's Progress* Harmondsworth, 1965

Catholic Encyclopedia New York, 1907-14

Chadwick, Henry *The Early Church* rev. ed. London, 1993

Chaucer, Geoffrey *The Canterbury Tales* (trans. Nevill Coghill) Harmondsworth, 1951

Cragg, G. R. *The Church and the Age of Reason* Harmondsworth, 1960

Davies, Horton and Marie-Hélène *Holy Days and Holidays* London and Toronto 1982

Dickinson, J.C. *The Shrine of Our Lady of Walsingham* Cambridge, 1956

Duffy, Eamon *The Stripping of the Altars* New Haven and London, 1992

Erasmus, Desiderius *The Colloquies Vol. III* (trans. N. Bailey) London, 1900

Fabri, Felix *The Wanderings of Felix Fabri* (trans. A Stewart) London 1892–97

Finlay, Ian *Columba* Glasgow, 1990

Finucane, R. C. *Miracles and Pilgrims: Popular Beliefs in Medieval England* London, 1977

Fletcher, Richard *The Conversion of Europe* London, 1998

Gillett, H. M. *Walsingham* London, 1950

Gonzalez Balado, J.L. *The Story of Taizé* London, 1980

Green, V.H.H. *Luther and the Reformation* London, 1964

Haffert, John M. *Meet the Witnesses* Fatima, 1961

Hanbury-Tenison, Robin *Spanish Pilgrimage* London, 1990

Harbison, Peter *Pilgrimage in Ireland* London, 1991

Harris, Ruth *Lourdes* London, 1999

Hartley, C. G. *The Story of Santiago de Compostela* London, 1912

Heath, Sidney *In the Steps of the Pilgrims* London, 1950

Hibbert, Christopher *The Grand Tour* London, 1987

Hogarth, James (trans.) *The Pilgrim's Guide: A 12th-Century Guide for the Pilgrim to St James of Compostella* London, 1992

Hopkins, Keith *A World Full of Gods* London, 2000

Hughes, Harry *Croagh Patrick* Westport, 1991

Hughes, Kathleen *The Church in Early Irish Society* London, 1966

— 'The Changing Theory and Practice of Irish Pilgrimage', *The Journal of Ecclesiastical History* Vol. 11, 1966

Hunt, E. D. *Holy Land Pilgrimage in the Later Roman Empire, AD 312–460* Oxford, 1982

Jackson, Bernard *Places of Pilgrimage* London, 1989

Kempis, Thomas à *The Imitation of Christ* Harmondsworth, 1952

Jusserand, J. *English Wayfaring Life in the Middle Ages* London, 1889

Kempe, Margery *The Book of Margey Kempe* (ed. W. Butler-Bowdon) London, 1936

Kendall, Alan *Medieval Pilgrims* London, 1970

Knight, Cher Krause 'Mickey, Minnie, and Mecca' in *Reclaiming the Spiritual in Art* (ed. Dawn Perlmutter and Debra Koppman) New York, 1999

Knox, E. A. *John Bunyan* London, 1928

Lehane, Brendan *Early Celtic Christianity* London, 1968

Luard, Nicholas *The Field of the Star* London, 1998

Masson, Georgina *The Companion Guide to Rome* London, 1965

McNeill, F. Marian *An Iona Anthology* Iona, 1990

— *Iona: A History of the Island* London, 1959

Miller, William *Mediaeval Rome* London, 1901

Mullins, E. *The Pilgrimage to Santiago* London, 1974

Neame, Alan *The Happening at Lourdes* London, 1968

Neary, Tom *I Saw Our Lady* Knock, 1995

Neillands, Rob *The Road to Compostela* Ashbourne, 1985

Ní Mheara, Róisín *In Search of Irish Saints* Blackrock, 1994

Ohler, Norbert *The Medieval Traveller* Woodbridge, 1989

Parks, G. B. *The English Traveller to Italy Vol. 1: The Middle Ages* Rome, 1954

Prescott, H. F. M. *Jerusalem Journey* London, 1954

Seward, Desmond *The Dancing Sun* London, 1993

Thomas, Keith *Religion and the Decline of Magic* London 1991

Snowden Ward, H. *The Canterbury Pilgrimages* London, 1927

Stevenson, J. *The Catacombs* London, 1978

Sumption, Jonathan *Pilgrimage: An Image of Mediaeval Religion* London, 1975

Taylor, J. E. *Christians and the Holy Places* Oxford, 1993

The Travels of Sir John Mandeville New York, 1964

Turner, V. and E. *Image and Pilgrimage in Christian Culture* New York, 1978

Walsh, William Thomas *Our Lady of Fatima* New York, 1990

Warner, Marina *Alone of All Her Sex* London, 1976

Webb, Diana *Pilgrims and Pilgrimage in the Medieval West* London, 1999

Westwood, Jennifer *Sacred Journeys* London, 1997

Wilkinson, John *Jerusalem Pilgrims Before the Crusades* Warminster, 1972

— *Jerusalem Pilgrimage 1099–1185* London, 1988

Williams, Wes *Pilgrimage and Narrative in the French Renaissance* Oxford, 1998

INDEX

ACKNOWLEDGMENTS

PHOTOGRAPHIC ACKNOWLEDGMENTS
For permission to reproduce the images on the following pages and for supplying photographs, the Publishers thank those listed below.

AKG, London: 46 (Universitätsbibliothek, Göttingen), 92 (Musée Condé, Chantilly), 123, 131 (Schlossmuseum, Weimar), 143, 159

AKG, London/British Library: 41; **Paul Almasy** 128–9, 178; **Erich Lessing** 5 (Museo Nazionale Romano delle Terme, Rome), 14–15 (S. Apollinare Nuovo, Ravenna), 17 (Musée Lapidaire, Arles), 20, 23, 31 (Kunsthistorisches Museum, Vienna), 32 (St George's Church, Madaba), 50 (Cathedral Treasury, Aachen), 64 (Museo di San Marco, Florence), 69 (Saint-Priest Church, Gimel-les-Cascades), 80 (Kunsthistorisches Museum, Vienna), 119 (Biblioteca Nazionale Marciana, Venice), 131 (Musée du Louvre, Paris); **Paul M. R. Maeyaert** 71 (Abbey Sainte-Foy, Conques); **Gilles Mermet** 2–3, 98

Ancient Art & Architecture Collection: 53, 63, 85, 110

©AXIOM: 105 (Chris Bradley), 120 (E. Simanor)

Bridgeman Art Library: 24 (San Francesco, Arezzo), 61 (Bibliothèque Nationale, Paris), 88 (Museum of London), 90–91 (Stapleton Collection), 116 (British Library, London), 126 (British Library, London), 139 (private collection), 141 (Roy Miles Fine Paintings, London)

Collections/ John D. Beldom: 165; **Ashley Cooper** 171; **Michael Diggin** 149; **Mike Kipling** 134; **Michael StMaur Sheil** 106, 109, 113, 157; **Geray Sweeney** 152

©Joe Cornish: 36, 55, 56-57, 86, 103, 154

Werner Forman Archive: 29

©Sonia Halliday Photographs: 8, 144 (F. H. C. Birch)

James Harpur: 172

©Magnum Photographs/Bruno Barbey: 162; **Richard Kalvar** 12, 176, 179; **Ferdinando Scianna** 7, 146

SCALA: 22, 72 (S. Anastasia, Verona), 77 (Prado, Madrid), 95 (S. Pietro, Vatican)

PUBLISHER'S ACKNOWLEDGMENTS
Commissioning editor Ginny Surtees
Project editor Fiona Robertson
Picture editor Sue Gladstone
Editorial assistance Michael Brunström
Designer Becky Clarke
Index Marie Lorimer
Production Antonia Parkin